1 3 5 7 9 10 8 6 4 2

Vintage
20 Vauxhall Bridge Road,
London SW1V 2SA

Vintage Classics is part of the Penguin Random House
group of companies whose addresses can be found at
global.penguinrandomhouse.com

 Penguin
Random House
UK

Restoration was first published in Great Britain by Hamish Hamilton in 1989
The Gustav Sonata was first published in Great Britain by
Chatto & Windus in 2016
This edition published by Vintage in 2018

penguin.co.uk/vintage

A CIP catalogue record for this book is available from the British Library

ISBN 9781784874032

Typeset in 9.5/14.5 pt FreightText Pro
by Jouve (UK), Milton Keynes
Printed and bound by Clays Ltd, St Ives plc

Penguin Random House is committed to a sustainable future for
our business, our readers and our planet. This book is made from
Forest Stewardship Council® certified paper.

Friendship
ROSE TREMAIN

VINTAGE MINIS

Introduction

THE SUBJECT OF romantic love has been fiction's prime obsession ever since Heathcliff called to Cathy from the Yorkshire moors, ever since the faithless Willoughby broke Marianne Dashwood's heart – and long before. And it's easy to see why. As people in the West believe less and less in religious salvation, so they seek meaning and redemption, happiness and comfort in union with a beloved other. That this search may sometimes engender jealousy, pain and disappointment only adds to its fatal attraction as a subject for the novelist.

I've added my bit to the vast store of literature about love in several of my books, but I have also paid close attention to love's quieter relation – friendship. For it's my belief that friendship, which often begins in early childhood and follows us all through our lives, is a formative and precious thing, able to influence our moral positioning in the world, teach us the rules of kindness and generosity, and anchor us to sanity when times are bad.

This small book traces two significant friendships: the bond between Robert Merivel and John Pearce in *Restoration*, and that between Gustav Perle and Anton Zwiebel in *The Gustav Sonata*.

It was interesting to note that in the 1995 movie of *Restoration*, the producers felt that the primary subject the novel explores, namely the bond between Merivel and Pearce – forever in conflict with Merivel's helpless adoration of the King and the material blessings his power can bestow – wasn't a strong enough theme for the film. They rewrote the story to give centrality to the role of Celia, the youngest of the King's mistresses, Merivel's 'paper bride' whom he is forbidden to touch.

Celia is placed in my book as the agent of Merivel's downfall. She serves the arc of the story, but emotionally, she isn't important. What Merivel feels for her is simple forbidden lust. What he feels for Pearce is not only lifelong affection; he also understands that Pearce is the living embodiment of his own conscience, that only in Pearce's stern heart resides any true knowledge of what he, Merivel, is, what he has been and what he could become. Merivel's persistent failure to live up to Pearce's vision is the engine that drives the narrative. It is through these multiple failures that we get to know Merivel: his acts of generosity, his talents as a doctor, his weakness for material splendour, his moments of repentance and self-laceration. It is also where much of the humour of the novel resides. In downgrading the friendship between

Merivel and Pearce to an incoherent sub-story, the movie writers literally lost the plot.

No film has yet been made of *The Gustav Sonata*. It would be difficult to realise, because this story traces a friendship that lasts for sixty years. We meet the boys at a kindergarten in Switzerland when they are five years old, and what is set down straight away is Gustav's instantaneous longing to make Anton his friend.

Anton's life, as the talented and emotional son of rich and affectionate Jewish parents, differs in almost all respects from Gustav's. Gustav is the lonely, neglected son of a hard-hearted single mother, given no toys, no physical nurturing, no encouragement, and only told repeatedly that he must practise 'self-mastery'. What he sees in Anton is a child who is free, who can become what he wishes to become, with the blessing of everyone around him.

It is as though, for Gustav, Anton has something god-like about him, an aura of wonder and power. By attaching himself to Anton, never able to let that attachment fade or die, Gustav will suffer much heartache. But he intuits early on that the other boy has a deep need of him, and that eventually, he may be the one person who will stand between Anton and his wilful self-destruction. This task, too, can sometimes be the duty of a friend.

I have tried to make coherent the trajectory of these friendships in the extracts from *Restoration* and *The*

Gustav Sonata that follow. Inevitably, there are ellipses in both stories – events taking place 'offstage' where we can't see them. But it's my belief that readers are much cleverer than some authors assume, and that here, they will enjoy the process of filling in the gaps.

Restoration

The beating heart

AT CAIUS COLLEGE, Cambridge, in 1647, I met my poor friend, Pearce.

His room was below mine on the cold stairway. We were both by then students of anatomy and, though our natures are so antipathetic, our rejection of Galenic theory, coupled with our desire to discover the precise function of each part of the body in relation to the whole, formed a bond between us.

One evening, Pearce came up to my room in a state of hilarious perturbation. His face, habitually grey-toned and flaky, was rubicund and damp, his stern green eyes suddenly afflicted with a louche brightness. 'Merivel, Merivel,' he babbled, 'come down to my room. A person is standing in it who has a visible heart!'

'Have you been drinking, Pearce?' I asked. 'Have you broken your vow of No Sack?'

'No!' exploded Pearce. 'Now come down and you will

see for yourself this extraordinary phenomenon. And, for a shilling, the person says he will permit us to touch it.'

'Touch his heart?'

'Yes.'

'It's not a cadaver then, if its mind is on money?'

'Now come, Merivel, before he flees into the night and is lost to our research for all eternity.'

(Pearce, I report in parentheses, has this flowery, sometimes melodramatic way of speaking that is interestingly at odds with the clipped, odourless and self-denying man he is. I often feel that no anatomical experiment would be capable of discovering the function of these ornate sentences in relation to the whole, soberly-dressed person, unless it is a universal but contradictory fact about Quakers that, whereas their gait, habit and ritual are monotonous and plain, their heads are secretly filled with a rapturous and fandangling speech.)

We descended to Pearce's room, where a fire was burning in the small grate. In front of the fire stood a man of perhaps forty years. I bade him good evening, but he only nodded at me.

'Shall I unbutton?' he asked Pearce.

'Yes!' said Pearce, his voice choking with anticipation. 'Unbutton, Sir!'

I watched as the man took off his coat and lace collar and began loosening his shirt. He let the shirt fall to the floor. Bound to his chest, and covering his heart, was a steel plate. Pearce, at this moment, took a handkerchief from his sleeve and mopped his moist brow. The man removed the plate, under which was a wad of linen, a little stained with pus.

Carefully, he unbound the linen and revealed to us a large hole in his breast, about the size of a Pippin apple, in the depths of which, as I leaned forward to look more closely at it, I saw a pink and moist fleshy substance, moving all the time with a regular pulse.

'See?' exclaimed Pearce, the heat of whose excited body seemed to fill the room with a tropical dampness. 'See it retract and thrust out again? We are witnessing a living, beating heart!'

The man smiled and nodded. 'Yes,' he said. 'A fracture of my ribs, occasioned by a fall from my horse two years ago, was brought to a terrible suppuration, voiding such a quantity of putrefaction that my doctors feared it would never heal. It did, however. You can see the sconce of the old ulcer at the edge of the hole here. But its ravages were so deep as to expose the organ beneath.'

I was dumbfounded. To observe, in a living being, standing nonchalantly by a fire, as if about to welcome friends for a few rounds of Bezique, the systole and diastole of his heart affected me profoundly. I began to understand why Pearce was in such a lather of excitement. But then – and this is why I set down the incident as a possible beginning to the story now unfolding round me – Pearce produced a shilling from the greasy leather purse in which he kept his pitiful worldly income and gave it to the stranger, and the man took it and said: 'You may touch it if you wish.'

I let Pearce go first. I saw his thin, white hand creep forwards and tremblingly enter the thoracic cavity. The man remained still and smiling. He didn't flinch. 'You may,' he said to Pearce, 'put your hand around the heart and exert gentle pressure.'

Pearce's thin mouth dropped open. Then he swallowed and withdrew his hand. 'I cannot do that, Sir,' he stammered.

'Then perhaps your friend will?' said the man.

I rolled back the lace at my wrist. Now, my own hand was shaking. I remembered that, just prior to Pearce's appearance in my room, I had cast two pieces of coal onto my fire and hadn't washed my hands since, but only wiped them carelessly on the seat of my breeches. I examined my palm for coal dust. It was faintly smudged with grey. I licked it and rubbed it again on my velvet buttocks. The open-hearted man watched me with an utter lack of concern. At my elbow, Pearce, in his vaporous dampness, was breathing irritatingly through his mouth.

My hand entered the cavity. I opened my fingers and, with the same care I had applied, as a boy, to the stealing of eggs from birds' nests, took hold of the heart. Still, the man showed no sign of pain. Fractionally, I tightened my grip. The beat remained strong and regular. I was about to withdraw my hand when the stranger said: 'Are you touching the organ, Sir?'

'Yes,' I said, 'don't you feel the pressure of my fingers?'

'No. I feel nothing at all.'

Pearce's breathing, at my side, was rasping, like that of

a hounded rodent. A pearl of sweat teetered on the tip of his pink nose. And my own mind was now forced to contemplate an astounding phenomenon: I am encircling a human heart, a living human heart with my hand. I am now, in fact, squeezing it with controlled but not negligible force. And the man suffers no pain whatsoever.

Ergo, the organ we call the heart and which is defined, in our human consciousness, as the seat – or even deified as the throne – of all powerful emotion, from unbearable sorrow to ecstatic love, is in itself utterly without feeling.

I withdrew my hand. I felt as full of trouble as my poor Quaker friend, to whom I would have turned for a tot of brandy, except that I knew he never had any. So while our visitor calmly strapped on his linen pad and his steel plate and stooped to pick up his shirt, Pearce and I sat down on his extremely hard settle and were, for a good few minutes, devoid of words.

From that day, I was unable to have the same reverence for my own heart as other men have for theirs.

Differences of opinion

IT IS INTERESTING to note the ease with which I had let my faith fall from me. Any love I had hitherto felt for God, I had given to the King, who had reciprocated (not as God had done, by speaking through the mouths of fat bishops and having frequent recourse to long periods of enigmatic silence) by laughing at my jokes and giving me royal kisses far sweeter to me than any embrace I'd had from any woman. It was the absence of these tender expressions of friendship and affection that had plunged me into such despair and sent me scrabbling about in the darkness once more, in search of my lost Redeemer, however cruel He might turn out to be.

This search of mine, these glow-worm prayers I sent out into the starry sky above Meg Storey's roof, if they failed to bring God back to comfort me, did, after a few weeks, send me my old friend, Pearce, who arrived at Bidnold on a mule. Strapped to the mule's back, were Pearce's pitiful worldly possessions (referred to by me, rather wittily, I think, as his 'burning coals', in reference to a mad Quaker at Westminster who had wandered about calling the fops to repentance with a dish of the said coals balanced on his head). What Pearce owned, in fact, was the following: three Bibles, one copy of his beloved Harvey's *De Generatione Animalium,* various other anatomical tracts, including works by Vesalius and da Vinci and Needham's *Disquisitio Anatomica De Formato Foetu,* some quill pens, a black coat and hat, two pairs of black breeches, some torn shirts and stockings, a box of rusty surgical instruments, a single pewter mug and plate and a china soup ladle made in Lancashire. This ladle was the only legacy of his mother, who had died in poverty to send Pearce to Cambridge. Sometimes, in the melancholy moods that so frequently afflict him, Pearce would hold the ladle close to his body and let his long fingers caress its cold surface, in the manner of a lute player plucking a living tune from its dead, hollowed wood.

I was glad, I will admit, to see Pearce. When Will Gates informed me that a man with a long neck and dressed in black was coming up the drive on a mule, I knew it could be none other than my old friend and former fellow-student and I ran out to greet him.

It was drizzling slightly and both Pearce and the mule appeared wet and muddy.

'We have come from the Fens,' he announced in his voice of doom.

'From the Fens, Pearce?' I said. 'What were you doing there?'

'I am a Fenlander now, Merivel,' he said. 'My work and life are there.'

'I notice that you put them in that order, Pearce: work first, life second.'

'Naturally. Except that the two are inseparable.'

'Well, I do not work at all, except a little painting.'

'Painting? How peculiar.'

'You've left the Royal College, then?'

'Yes. I work only with the insane. Take the mule, will you, and see she's fed? We're both very weak.'

Pearce then dismounted, staggered a pace or two and fell to his knees. I shouted for Will Gates, who came running like a bullet, and together he and I helped Pearce into the house. I asked the groom to rescue the 'burning coals' quickly, before the mule died and rolled over on the soup ladle.

We put Pearce to bed in the least colourful of my rooms, the Olive Room, a north-facing bedchamber, in

which I had left intact some dark panelling and had cur-
tained the bed in a sombre green, only enlivened by a little
crimson fringe. Here, after drinking some venison broth
and enquiring whether his books could be sent up to him,
he fell into a sleep that lasted thirty-seven hours. During
most of this time, I stayed at his bedside, checking his
pulse now and then, listening to his breathing, dozing a
little and sipping claret and staring at his elongated grey
face, which I found at once so irritating and yet so inex-
pressibly dear to me.

When he woke up at last, I was anxious to tell him of
the despair into which I had fallen and to see whether he
could suggest any remedy. But he had, it turned out, made
the arduous journey on the mule from the Fens for one
reason only: to reveal to me that he had found, in his work
with the mad people of what he called the New Bedlam,
located somewhere between Waterbeach and Whittlesea,
a deep and profound sense of peace, and to try to per-
suade me to leave my life of 'vanity and show' to join him
in his labours.

'I sense,' he said, staring at my freckled, ruddy and
bewigged visage, 'that you're not at ease, Merivel. The
light has gone out of your eyes. Luxury is suffocating your
vital flame.'

I looked down. Though I had a terrible urge to confess
to Pearce, amid childlike tears, that it was not luxury that
had robbed me of my happiness, but the King's abandon-
ment of me, and that I was indeed a desperate man,
though not at all for the reasons he surmised, I refrained

from doing so, knowing that it would only lead Pearce into more flowery discussion of how the insane are the innocent of the earth, and how, only by succouring them 'like little children' can we be saved.

'Thank you, Pearce, for your concern,' I said, 'but you are completely wrong. If my eyes appear a little lacklustre, it's merely because I have watched at your bedside for a great quantity of time with hardly any sleep. As to my vital flame, it is burning very brightly.'

'I know you, Merivel. When you stood in my room in Caius and put your hand on that man's heart, then it was burning!'

'Indeed! And if you had seen me in the park the other day with my oil paints –'

'You hope to find salvation in art?'

'I'm not speaking necessarily of salvation . . .'

'But I am, Merivel. For is not death the supreme moment of mortal existence, the hour in which we reap what we have sown?'

'You choose to see it like that, Pearce.'

'No. I do not choose. The Lord tells me it is so. And what are you sowing, Merivel, here in your palace?'

'It's merely a manor, Pearce.'

'No! It's a palace! And full of iniquity, if these scarlet tassels are anything to go by.'

'They're nothing to go by.'

'Answer me, Merivel. What are you *sowing*?'

Again, I looked down. The agricultural metaphors with which the Bible is strewn have always struck me as simplistic and crude, but I particularly did not like Pearce's repeated emphasis on the word 'sowing', for it somehow evoked in my mind my letter to the King, which had been intended as a seed in the forgetful Royal brain, but which had indubitably fallen upon stony ground.

I looked up at Pearce, white and gaunt on his white pillow.

'Colour,' I said. 'Colour and light. I am sowing these.'

'What pagan, freakish piffle you do spout, Merivel!'

'No,' I said. 'Have a little faith, Pearce. Through colour and light, I hope to arrive at art. Through art, I hope to arrive at compassion. And through compassion, though the journey may be a deal more terrible than the one you've just undertaken – your mule is dead by the way – I hope to arrive at enlightenment.'

'Enlightenment,' said Pearce with a sniff, 'is not enough.'

'Perhaps. But sufficient to be going on with.'

Before Pearce could comment upon this, I plucked his ladle off a walnut escritoire, where a servant had placed it, and handed it to him.

'Here is your ladle,' I said. 'Play upon it quietly, until you feel restored enough to venture downstairs, where I have something of great beauty to show you.'

'What is it?' asked Pearce, suspiciously.

'An Indian Nightingale,' I replied. And before Pearce could make some disdainful comment about my bird, I left his room.

* * *

I WILL NOW tell you that it had become my daily habit to sing a little to my Indian Nightingale. I have no voice at all, and so flat do the notes come out that Minette, in her brief life, used to howl and whimper the moment I opened my mouth, as if I were a desert dog from the Land of Mar. But, my lack of talent notwithstanding, I love singing. I hear the right notes in my head. The fact that I can seldom attain them distresses my listeners, but doesn't seem to upset me in the least. I am, in this respect, like a man trying to fling his body over a five-barred gate and, no matter how spirited his run or ready his heart, finding himself at each attempt still on the wrong side of it and yet nonetheless filled with joy at his efforts. Finn had told me to play the oboe to the bird, and I had sent to London for one of these instruments but, in the meantime, I sang to it, rather quietly so as not to affront it, and it regarded me watchfully, moving its tail up and down and letting fall onto the painted base of the cage tiny filaments of shit.

When at last Pearce rose from his bed and arrived in my Withdrawing Room dressed in his greasy black clothes, he found me singing to my nightingale. Shading his eyes from the brilliance of the furnishings, he approached the cage and stood blinking at it like a lizard. I ceased my singing and the bird at once let out a melodious trill.

'I recognise that,' said Pearce.

'What is it?' I asked excitedly. 'Something by Purcell?'

'No,' said Pearce, and turned upon me a pitying, reptilian look. 'That is the warble of a common blackbird.'

'Don't be foolish, Pearce,' I said at once, meanwhile recognising that my heart, all unfeeling as I know it to be, had started to beat erratically. 'The bird was a gift to me. That creature has travelled the oceans.'

'When? Who brought it?'

'I have no idea. An ornithologist, no doubt. It has been round Cape Horn. So let us have no more talk of blackbirds!'

Pearce shrugged and turned away from the cage, as if it was of no further interest to him whatsoever. 'You've been duped, Merivel,' was all he said.

'Very well,' I said. 'We will go out into the garden and find a blackbird and listen to its feeble song, and you will see that you're wrong.'

'As you wish,' said Pearce, 'but I would remind you that it is winter and birds do not sing a great deal at this time of year.'

'Further proof, then, that this is not an English bird. You just heard its lovely trill.'

'No doubt it mistook its surroundings for a flower bed.'

I smiled at Pearce. The insult he'd intended to my gaudy room in fact pleased me a great deal, and I mention to you, in passing, that Pearce's criticisms of me do not inevitably have the humbling effect upon me that they so strenuously desire.

Pearce and I then put on our cloaks (his so exceedingly threadbare that an irritating shiver of pity ran through me) and went out into the December morning, filigree'd with frost, sparkling and silent in the dry, icy air.

We stood still and listened. Some way off in the park, rooks were circling and cawing above the beech trees, but there was scarcely another sound at all. 'Let's walk down the drive a little,' I suggested, and we set off at the slow pace always adopted by Pearce, who, if God himself were suddenly to appear before him with open arms, would, I believe, forbear to run, but approach his Maker with his habitual measured and ungainly step.

After we had gone a very little way, a sound I had not expected at all began to clatter and jingle in the frosty quiet. It was the sound of a coach and four. I caught my breath. Without any doubt, it would be Violet Bathurst riding over for a little mulled claret and an hour in my bed, and here was I listening out for blackbirds with the one friend whose mind would be tormented by her arrival. I knew, if I wished to keep Pearce at Bidnold, I would have to send Violet away, however beguiling the thought of her company might be.

We stepped to one side as the coach came on, but as it rounded the curve in the drive, I saw immediately that the beautiful greys which pulled it were not Violet's horses. I was expecting no other guests and couldn't imagine who could be coming to my house at such a gallop.

I put out an arm and the coachman (recognising me by my fine clothes as the master of Bidnold) attempted to slow the horses. But their canter had been so brisk that they and the coach had gone past me before they could be pulled up, and all I had was a fleeting glimpse of a woman's face at the carriage window, shrouded in what appeared to be a black veil.

The coach had now arrived in front of the main doorway. With Pearce trailing me, like the ghost of the exiled John Loseley, I started to run towards the house, unfortunately slipping in my haste on an icy patch of the driveway, falling down in a most humiliating fashion, tearing my peach-coloured stockings and grazing my right hand.

I got up and stumbled on. 'Ho there!' I called. 'Hello!' But when I arrived, puffing and flushed, at my doorway, I saw that the occupant of the coach had already gone inside the house and that some large boxes and trunks were now being carried in by my footmen.

Noticing with great vexation that my hand was bleeding, I walked into my hallway. After the bright, cold sunlight, it appeared very dark, and indeed I could at first see no one at all. Then I looked up. Standing on the oak stairs was the woman in the black veil. Her stance was strangely familiar to me and, even as she reached up and flung back the veil, I knew whose face I was about to see. It was the face of my wife.

We stood staring at each other. Her stare – notwithstanding my crimson cheeks and my wig fallen over my eyebrows – was far more terrible than mine. She seemed to have aged almost out of time. Her small face, dimpled and pretty in my memory, looked grey and gaunt and her eyes were swollen and red, as if she had been crying day and night since the beginning of winter. I moved forward a pace. I wanted, in my pity for her, to say her name, but realised, even as I opened my mouth, that I couldn't remember what it was.

DURING MY FANCIFUL and hectic redecorations at Bidnold, I had allowed myself to ignore the possibility that Celia Clemence would one day take up habitation under its roof.

Thus, although the house contained eleven bedchambers, none, in my mind, had been furnished for the woman Violet Bathurst jealously referred to as 'Lady Merivel, Your Bride', but whose continuing existence was invariably absent from my mind. 'Listen, Violet,' I was in the habit of saying on the occasion of my Lady B's envious outbursts. 'I am no more conscious of Celia as my lawful wife than Bathurst is of you as his. Rest assured that I never think of her.'

Usually, Violet's jealousy would be assuaged by this statement, but one evening, even as I knelt over her and gently eased my tumescent member along the soft furrow between her breasts, she suddenly reached up and pushed me sideways, so that I would have fallen onto the floor had my right leg not been tangled in the sheet. 'Your analogy with Bathurst,' she said crossly 'is misleading and, if deliberately so, then you are a cruel and cynical man. For as you well know, Merivel, Bathurst has moments of remembering and at such times becomes importunate. On Wednesday night, for instance, lucidity returned to him in the middle of supper and he began crawling towards me on his hands and knees under the Dining Room table, the while unbuttoning himself. If I had not quickly reminded him that his brace of woodcock – his favourite game – were getting cold on his plate, I simply do not know what might have happened. And so it may be with you, Merivel. That which you swear you have forgotten, you will one day come grovelling towards.'

'Violet,' I said, recovering my kneeling position (only disconcerted very mildly by the similarity of my stance to Bathurst's under the table), 'grovelling is a thing I have done but once in my life, when I inadvertently fell over at the King's feet. The notion that I will ever, as long as I am of sound mind, grovel to Celia is a pure fiction, not to be entertained for one second more!'

I put my mouth upon Violet's at this moment, thus preventing further speech, and the evening proceeded very pleasantly, Violet's sudden attack of jealousy having roused her to a wild and shameless abandon.

But even as I saw her into her coach, I found myself remembering Celia and wondering where, in the unlikely event of her unexpected arrival at Bidnold, I would lodge her. Had I not, on my strange wedding night, witnessed the immodest thrusting of her loins towards the King's mouth and heard through the closet door a wailing of pleasure worthy of an African wildcat, I would have believed Celia to be an entirely chaste and modest person, a person of sober taste and small appetite, finding comfort and contentment in a bedchamber hung, say, with pale apricot moiré and ornamented by sombre prints of rivers and cathedrals. As it was, by the time I had ceased waving to Violet's gloved hand disappearing into the night, I had already decided that what I called the Marigold Room would be the one I would offer to Celia. Late as the hour was, I had my servants go up and light candles in the Marigold Room, so that I could take a look at it. I would have given the thing no thought at all but for Violet. For this one brief night, she had awoken in me a minute flicker of excitement at the idea of my wife's arrival. The next morning, however, Celia was once more consigned to that part of my brain I imagine to be like a coiled fistula, filled not with putrescent matter, but with utter darkness and into which so much of what I have once known is carefully crammed.

Now, HERE I am, in my torn stockings and with my bleeding hand, staring at my poor wife as she turns to me on the stairway and I read in her face some terrible calamity. 'My dear!' I burst out, whipping from my pocket a plum-coloured silk handkerchief and fumblingly binding my hand with it. 'Welcome to Bidnold! If you had given me a little warning, I would have made everything ready for you.'

'I need no welcome,' says Celia, and her voice is reedy, like the voice of an old dying crone. 'The servants will show me to my room.'

'Yes,' I stammer, 'or I will show you. It's to be the Marigold Room . . .'

My hand is bound now, but as I take hold of the banister rail and prepare to mount the stairs towards her, I see her recoil from me, as from some rearing viper. 'Stay away!' she whispers, seemingly faint with revulsion. 'Please stay away.'

I stop at once and smile at her kindly. 'Celia,' I say, remembering her name at last, 'you need have no fear of me whatsoever. I will never ask anything of you. All I wanted was to show you to your room, the colours and furnishings of which I hope may be of some comfort to you in whatever misfortune –'

'The servants will show me. Where is my woman, Sophia?'

'What?' I say.

'Where is my woman? Where is Sophia?'

'I have no idea. Did you bring her with you? She's your maid?'

'Yes. Call her please, Merivel.'

I turn and look towards the front door. Two grooms are stumbling through it with a leather trunk, filled no doubt with ermine-trimmed bonnets and newt-skin shoes bought for his Dear One by my sometime master, the King. My mind is travelling in sudden sorrow towards a certain set of striped dinner napkins, now unused but kept folded in linen in an oaken chest, when I suddenly see Pearce, panting and wheezing like his late mule, arrive in my hall.

'Ah, Pearce,' I say quickly. 'Have you caught sight of a woman named Sophia?'

Pearce is blinking. His huge eyes, his prehensile nose and his long neck make him, on the instant, resemble a species of nocturnal tree-climbing animals I have seen described as marsupials (a strange word).

'No,' says Pearce. 'What is occurring, Merivel? I scent some misfortune.'

'Yes,' I say, 'misfortune there does seem to be. But for now we must find my wife's woman . . .'

'Your *wife* is come?'

'Yes. Here she is. Go out to her carriage please, Pearce, and tell her maid that her mistress calls.'

Pearce is wiping his eyes on his threadbare cloak, the better to believe that the ghostly woman in black is indeed Celia Clemence, last glimpsed by him laughing merrily at her wedding. I am about to urge him outside once more when a buxom, ugly, dark-haired woman of perhaps thirty-five appears, carrying two or three dresses in her arms.

'Sophia,' Celia calls hoarsely, 'come up.'

Sophia looks from Pearce to me, seems immediately affronted by the sight of us both and so goes swiftly up the stairs to where her mistress is reaching out her hand.

At my side, emerged from I know not where, I now find Will Gates.

'Will,' I say with great urgency, 'please conduct my wife and her woman to the Marigold Room.'

'The Marigold Room, Sir?' whispers Will. 'Might I suggest another?'

'No, you might not,' I snap.

Will glares at me but nonetheless, like the matchless servant that he is, goes nimbly up the stairs past the two women and with his habitual unflowery courtesy leads them onwards and up. The grooms follow with the heavy trunks and boxes.

I DID NOT see Celia again that day.

After supper, which I took alone with Pearce, I enquired of my cook whether orders had come down for food. I was told that some *bouillon* and a plum tartlet had been sent up.

'Was it eaten?' I asked.

'Either that,' said my wall-eyed chef, Cattlebury, 'or the dog had it.'

'Dog?'

'Aye, Sir.'

'What dog, Cattlebury?'

'Mr Gates, Sir, says they brought in a dog, a small Spaniel like the one as died on you, Sir Robert.'

Ah, was my melancholy thought as I left the kitchen, the King is too cunning for us all! To those he knows he must one day abandon, he gives this sweet, living gift, just to be certain that our love for him remains with us (as if he could doubt that it would!) in case he may, at some future time, have need of us again. Poor Celia!

As I returned to my Study, where I had left Pearce reading some forgotten Latin text from my Padua days, I resolved that I must try, as soon as she would let me, to offer words of understanding and comfort, and in so doing perhaps find a little relief from my own despair. For there was no doubt in my mind now: the King had sent her away. She had played her part, just as I had once played mine, and now he had cast us off. I imagine him at dinner, his arm draped elegantly round Lady Castlemaine's white shoulders, the candlelight lending a seductive gloss to the little moustache he keeps so fastidiously trimmed. He leans towards Castlemaine, nibbles the emerald dangling from her ear. 'What do you know of Norfolk, Barbara?' he whispers.

'Very little,' she replies, 'except that it is far from London!'

'Precisely!' smiles the King, 'and therefore useful to me. It is there, you see, that I *envoie* all those I have begun to find tedious.'

'WELL,' I SAID to Pearce, as I sat down in the Study, 'I believe I know now for certain what has happened. What I greatly fear, however, is that Celia will believe her life is over. I really do not think she will ever be consoled.'

Pearce (as is one of his irritating habits, detested by me since our student days) did not so much as glance up from his book when I finished speaking, but simply read on, as if I had not even entered the room. I waited. Sometimes I find Pearce so deeply annoying that, were I the King, I would have bouts of wanting to send him to Norfolk.

'Pearce,' I said, 'did you hear what I said?'

'No,' said Pearce. 'I didn't. I imagine it was some observation on your wife's plight.'

'Yes, it was.'

'Well, I have nothing to add. Fools such as you have

become and courtesans such as she, once the whiplash of mirth or passion has died, invariably feel the scourge of the whip itself.'

I sighed. I opened my mouth to discourage Pearce from further muddled metaphorical utterances of this kind when he lifted the little book he'd been reading and brandished it in my face.

'*This* is interesting!' he announced. 'On the Cartesian question of spontaneous generation: "For if generation of the lower forms is not spontaneous, then *vermiculus unde venit*? Whence the maggot?"'

I got up. 'I'm sorry, Pearce,' I said, my voice brittle and cold, 'but I do not feel able, after the troubles of this day, to enter upon a discussion of maggots. I shall go and play my oboe until bedtime.'

With that I strode out and went to my Music Room. I shall spare you an account of my struggles with my instrument that evening and the quantity of anxious spittle with which reed after reed was saturated. I shall report only that I wrestled with simple scales for an hour or more, after which time my grazed hand was giving me so much pain that I lay down on the floor of the Music Room and put it between my thighs, with my knees drawn up to my stomach, and in this childlike posture fell into a troubled sleep.

When I awoke, very stiff and cold, with my hand swollen and set into a premature *rigor mortis,* I saw from the grey light at the window that the winter dawn was breaking over Norfolk, County of Exiles. Despite my numbness and pain, I found myself, on the instant of waking, filled with purpose and resolve. I must go immediately to Celia. I must make her understand that, stranger to her though I am, disagreeable though she may find my physical self, I am occasionally a person of generous mind and that – forswearing any hope of recompense or reward – I am content to be her protector and treat her with respect and kindness for as long as she remains at Bidnold.

I went up to my own chamber, where I changed my clothes and wig. None of the servants was yet stirring. By the handsome timepiece given to me by the King, I saw that it was a little before six. The embers of a fire were still glowing in my grate and I tried to warm my dead hand somewhat before setting out along the chilly corridors to the Marigold Room.

I stopped in front of Celia's door. I could hear a tiny, piteous sound, which I first took to be weeping, but then recognised all too foolishly well as the whimpering of a Spaniel. Minette, Minette, I thought. I grieve for you. You are buried in the park and the deer chomp the grass above you . . . But this was quite the wrong moment for self-pity, so I knocked with a firm and authorative hand (my left hand, the other one being now afflicted with a sudden intolerable pricking and tingling) and waited.

After a moment or two, an unfamiliar foreign-sounding voice, the voice of Sophia no doubt, called angrily: 'Who is there?'

'Sir Robert,' I replied, 'I want to speak to Lady Merivel, please.'

The dog was now scrabbling at the door. I believe the maid pushed it away roughly before she said: 'My mistress is sleeping. Go, please, away.'

'No,' I said. 'I will not go away. Please wake my wife. I have much that is important to say to her.'

'No!' hissed Sophia. 'My Lady is sleeping!'

'She may sleep later. I must speak to her now.'

I was about to add that at this precise moment I was feeling a great deal of compassion for Celia but that such is the nature of mood and emotion that I could not guarantee, if forced to return at another time, to find within me the same degree of kindness, when the door was opened. The maid stood there in her nightgown and lace cap. I saw now that her skin was sallow and her upper lip uncommonly hairy. I decided she must be one of the large retinue of Portuguese women who had been shipped to England with Catherine of Braganza, many of whom had found themselves forced to serve outside their beloved Queen's household and who, by the Whitehall gallants, were known scathingly as 'the Farthingales' after the peculiar hooped skirts beneath which they concealed their stocky legs.

This Sophia gave me a look of the utmost loathing as I went past her into the room. I shall be rid of you, Farthingale, I said to her in my mind, for I am master here.

I must relate, however, that in the scene which followed (I deliberately refer to it as a 'scene', for the albeit unoriginal notion that my life since my wedding has become something of a farce does very often strike me as

apt) I demonstrated all too lamentably my lack of master-
liness and found myself most horribly insulted and
abused. This is what happened:

I found Celia, not in bed as Farthingale had pretended,
but sitting on the orange and green cushions of the window seat, fully dressed in her black garb, staring out at the
dismal dawn.

I asked her if she had slept well and she replied that she
had not slept at all so hideous did she find the room, so
vulgar, so gaudy and tasteless. She could not, she said,
imagine anyone – except probably myself – being capable
of finding any rest within it.

Reminding myself that I should not become angry, I
assured her calmly that she was free to select another
room whenever she wished. I then asked her if I might sit
down. She answered that she would prefer me to remain
standing.

By this time disconcerted by Celia's hostility, of which
I truly believed myself undeserving, I nevertheless began
upon what I had come to say. I told Celia that I of all
people, who had briefly known some affection from the
King, understood exceedingly well the quality, the measure of her sadness. I began to speak of the terrible degree
to which my being and my spirit, once calm and content
in its serving of God and the Trinity, was now possessed
by the King. I went so far as to say that I believed there
was no man or woman in the Kingdom (be they as pious
as my dead parents, be they Puritan or Quaker, be they
lord or lunatic) utterly free from and untouched by any

longing to see their own putrid lives lit up by his radiance. 'Inevitably then,' I went on, 'you and I, Celia, who have known something of the man's love . . .'

'*Love?*' shrieked Celia. 'What presumption, Merivel! What self-deception! How can you dare to speak of what the King felt for you as love! Not for one second, not for one mote of time did King Charles love you, Merivel. I advise you never again to use the word!'

'My only intention . . .' I began, but Celia, now standing and fixing upon my face her fearful eyes, refused to let me speak. She jabbed a small white finger towards my scarlet waistcoat as she yelled: 'The truth is that the King, in his love for *me*, in his passion for *me*, made use of you. He used you, Merivel. He looked around for the stupidest man he could find, the densest, the most foolish, the one who would accept whatever he did like a dog and cause him no trouble – and he found you! I begged him, don't marry me to that idiot, I begged him on my knees, but all he did was laugh. "Who can I ask," he said, "to be paid cuckold *except* an idiot?" Do you understand, Merivel? Dense as you are, do you comprehend what I'm saying?'

Well, I'm afraid I cannot go on with the scene. It is very painful, is it not? Of course I 'comprehended', as she put it. I comprehended all too chillingly and although, in her rage and despair, she flung yet more insults at me, while the odious fat Farthingale looked on and smirked, I simply am not able to set them down.

I made no further attempt to offer my friendship to Celia, let alone enquire how the King's rejection of her had come about, but quietly withdrew from the room, shutting the door behind me before Farthingale could slam it in my face.

My first thought was: to whom, after this terrible revelation, shall I turn for comfort? To Pearce? To Will Gates? To Violet Bathurst? To Meg Storey? To my lost wench, Rosie Pierpoint? I felt a most terrible need of some kindly human company. But the hour was still early, my house dark, and I imagined them all sleeping: Pearce on his back with his white hands folded upon his ladle; Will Gates on his truckle bed dreaming of village girls; Violet enclosed by sumptuous brocade, safely absent from old Bathurst's brain; Meg in her attic, fallen asleep in her drawers and with beer upon her breath; sweet Rosie in Pierpoint's bed, stirring now to the murmur of the waking river . . . and I let them be.

I walked away from the Marigold Room to the west wing of the house and climbed the cold stone stairway to the circular room in the turret, whose discovery had given me so much joy. The room was still empty, still untouched. I went to each of the windows and looked out. A small slit of red in the sky hinted at sunrise. A white mist lay on the park, shrouding the deer.

I sat down under one of the windows. It will never be used now, this seemingly perfect room, I thought. At least, not by me. For it is surely the place which, though it aspires to do so, my mind can neither order nor understand. It is beyond my limit. I am earthbound, gross, ignorant. I will never reach to here.

* * *

IT WAS OF course Pearce to whom I eventually confided what had been said by Celia in the Marigold Room.

I had agreed to go with him upon a strange errand: to dig up a small quantity of earth from the village grave-yard, from which Pearce intended to extract the saltpetre. He is suffering, among other afflictions, from a bladder stone and hopes to dissolve it in time by swallowing regular doses of this foul substance.

For the purposes of gathering the earth, he had taken with us a small spade and a leather bag. With some chivalry (Pearce still being weak from his arduous journey across the Fens) I offered to carry the spade and Pearce hung the bag about his long neck, thus giving himself more than ever the air of a mendicant.

We walked slowly down the drive and out onto the little road that leads to the village. Once we had gathered the earth, it was my intention to offer Pearce some refreshment at the Jovial Rushcutters, over which I could tell him what had been said to me. I found, however, that so slow was the pace of Pearce's walk that I was forced to prattle to keep myself from getting cold and thus had come out with my sad story long before we had reached the village, finishing it by hurling the spade away from me in a violent gesture of anguish.

Pearce looked at me. In his large eyes, I did detect a small glimmer of pity, but for some time, during which I retrieved the spade, he walked on in silence. I was just beginning to wonder whether I should embark on my tale again, this time making certain every few sentences that he was listening to me, when Pearce cleared his throat and said:

'It is my belief, all unfashionable as I know it to be, that all things, including lunacy, may be susceptible to cure.'

'What?' I said.

'It has been believed since the beginning of time, that the mad are possessed of Devils and are thus filled with evil. This evil, it is universally agreed, must be beaten out of them by extreme chastisement, torture and all other conceivable kinds of cruelty . . .'

'Pearce,' I said, 'happy as I am to discuss your work at the New Bedlam at some later time I would ask you now to give your attention to my state of mind and—'

'I am giving my attention to your state of mind, Merivel. If you could, for once, listen to what I have to say instead of disregarding me, you will see that I have some helpful ideas on the subject.'

We walked on. A pale sun now emerged from behind a bank of cloud and glimmered eerily upon us.

'Let me describe to you,' Pearce went on, 'a woman who was brought to me at the Whittlesea Hospital – for such is the name we have given to our Bedlam. This woman had been found half drowned in a ditch after wandering the shire for month upon month, year upon year, begging and shouting obscene words, mortifying her body, particularly her breasts and her arms with sharp hawthorn twigs. Her chief delight, in her poor suffering mind, was to defile. She kept her own excrement in a pouch, with which to smear the hands and fine clothes of those who gave her alms; with the same substance she daubed tombstones and churches. When we took her in, so terrible was her rage that, though I do not like to see this done, we were forced to chain her limbs to the wall. And for several weeks, she fought night and day with her chains, so that her wrists and ankles became running sores, no matter how carefully we bound them with cloth. Do you begin to form a picture of this woman, Merivel?'

'Yes, thank you, Pearce,' I said.

'Very well. Let me recount to you then the morning upon which I went to this woman and found her quiet at last. She was sitting hunched in the corner, her limbs folded up and still. As I entered, she lifted her arm and pointed to two large turds she had recently voided onto the floor. I did not particularly wish to look at them, but her pointing was very insistent and the change in her demeanour so considerable that I did what she asked. And when I approached, I saw that writhing in and out of the greenish stools were two great worms, each several inches long, very white and loathsome. And then I looked again at the woman and she was weeping. And I unchained her and we took her away and washed her and put her in a clean bed. And from that day she was calm and talked with us of her home when she was a child and of the baby she had in her sister's care and we knew that she was cured. The worms had poisoned her blood and this poisoned blood had entered her brain. She was not wicked, Merivel. She was ill. Mercifully for her, her body at last discharged from itself the source of her illness.'

'I am glad for her,' I said flatly.

'And so to you, my dear friend. Now I shall tell you what I perceive has happened. You are possessed by one thought: you wish the King to draw you back to him and to love you. In the absence of this love, you are literally mad with grief. And in time this madness will work horribly in you, so that you will become, like the woman I've just spoken of, a defiler. True, you may not daub others with excrement, but you will daub them with hate. Unless you can come to see your ache for the King's favours as a morbid affliction of which you must rid yourself or die.'

Pearce stopped on the road and reached out and placed his bony hands on my shoulders. I opened my mouth to speak, but he went on:

'What happened this morning, those harsh words that were spoken, I can only see as beneficial, Merivel. Do not stop me, but listen! In this knowledge, the knowledge that the King has never loved you, only used you, as I long suspected, lies the only hope of your cure. For this knowledge must be the beneficial evacuation of nature, the rank and putrefied stool which, foul as it is, carries out and away the far fouler source of poison and decay – the great worm of hope.'

I stared at Pearce. I was unable to speak, so filled was I suddenly with belief in the rightness of what he had said. I could only nod my head and keep nodding it up and down, as if I were a stupid jester trying to jingle the bells on his hat.

* * *

SOME DAYS PASSED, during which I felt a welcome calm settle upon my spirits.

When Pearce informed me he must return to Whittlesea, I thanked him – with precisely the kind of sentimental profusion he so scorns in me – for saving me, before it was too late, from becoming a veritable lunatic and earnestly begged him to visit me again at Bidnold as soon as his work permitted. He replied that he would pray for me and urged me meanwhile to return to my medical books, 'in order,' as he put it 'to replace the world of acquisition with the world of knowledge'. I had not the heart to tell him that I did not feel capable of doing this. 'What I *can* promise you, Pearce,' I said, 'is that my foolish expectation with regard to all matters Royal is dead. I do not expect, as long as I live, to see the King again. Where my future lies, I cannot tell. In my painting, perhaps?'

I report here that Pearce's opinion of my pictures was very little higher than Finn's, but he made no comment upon this last statement, only busied himself with gathering up his 'burning coals' and placing them into a little tragic pile. In a sudden excess of affection for him, I offered to give him my horse, Danseuse, for his journey, but he refused, informing me that the mare was too strong and high-spirited for him and requesting me modestly to purchase a new mule for him.

One of my grooms was duly sent on this errand and returned with a speckled, ungainly creature, 'somewhat prone to bite, Sir Robert, but stout-hearted, Sir, for the long trek'.

I did not tell Pearce about the biting and the mule was straight away saddled up. Pearce mounted and without further word to me, trotted off down the drive. Just as he reached the first bend, I saw the animal throw its head round and attempt to snap at Pearce's foot. Pearce answered this insult with a kick to the mule's flank and man and beast shot off at a gallop, leaving behind them a small plume of dust, at which I stared until it settled.

His stumbling run

SINCE MY LAST glimpse of Pearce on the speckled mule, I had not given him a great deal of thought. He does not love or condone my follies. My behaviour towards Celia would have made him weep with shame. Thus, it was not comfortable to think of him while I was at the same time giving him cause for embarrassment and grief.

Now, cast out from Celia's life, and knowing I would soon saddle Danseuse and make my way to the Fens, I was able once again to set his palid visage before my mind's eye. It is a face most dear to me, yet one which creates in me – in equal measure – feelings of sorrow, irritation and tenderness. 'Tender' is a word of which Pearce makes considerable use, it being a Quaker term applied to those tolerant souls (and there are not very many of them, if Pearce is to be believed) who do not, at the sight of a Quaker, spit in his eye or demand that he take off his hat. I am 'tender' then. In our past together, I occasionally

It is a face most
dear to me, yet
one which creates
in me – in equal
measure – feelings
of sorrow, irritation
and tenderness.

stood between Pearce and his antagonists, not because I am courageous, but because Pearce has about him some innocence of a child and I do not like to see children hurt and insulted. Yet for all these acts of gallantry, Pearce is harsh with me. He once likened my life 'to a poorly done sampler, Merivel. Showing a variety of stitches, yet making up a most incoherent picture.' He is a man who, for all his rapturous speech, cannot bring himself to make visible the secret affections of his heart. I know that he loves me very dearly; he, I believe, does not know that he does. And yet, when I arrive at his wretched hospital, he will run (or at least increase the speed of his gait somewhat) to greet me. When he sees me, he will be glad.

There is little in our lives, since the day I went to Whitehall, to bind our friendship. And sometimes it appears to me as a ghostly thing, a thing which had its proper life in Cambridge in the years of the King's exile. These 'ghosts' were to be found very often together late at night, putting coal onto small fires, eating plum cake, trying at the same time to digest Descartes' theory that the ethereal human spirit was connected to the 'body machine' by the pineal gland; then giving up at last and spitting it out and giving in to laughter.

The ghost Pearce was sentimentally fond of fishing and in summer would take the ghost Merivel with him on his angling trips. 'The Apostles,' Pearce would say fancifully, as the two of them sat watching for mayfly, 'were fishermen. Fishing is a contemplative, devotional thing and not entirely suited to you, Merivel, who are too restless and dazzling.' And it is true, Pearce was the luckier angler. The brown trout came to his hook on the evening rise. Merivel got only the muddy grayling. But the ghosts stayed on the river, content with each other, content with the sport, till the air cooled and a thin mist began to sit on the water and they became shadowy in time. I can remember that returning to my room in Caius from these fishing expeditions was like returning from another world. And the memory of them, coming sometimes to my mind when it is vexed with trouble, has always been soothing.

So, endeavouring to put from me the devastations of the recent time, consigning to darkness the smell of the King's perfume, the sound of Celia's voice, the touch of the King's hand upon my nose, the sight of my own lust on my starlit roof, I looked at my remembrance of Pearce very closely, as it might be through a microscope, allowing that which had become invisible to be seen once more in clear definition. In this way, I prepared myself for my journey.

For my decision to go to the Fens ran some way ahead of my ability to do so. In short, no sooner had I said the word 'Pearce' out loud than I knew myself to be afraid. My friend's company I knew would be beneficial to me; the company of a hundred lunatics could afford me nothing but pain. Thus, I tarried at the Leg. From the ghosts by the trout stream, I begged courage.

THE DATE OF my setting forth was the tenth of March.

I passed the first night at Puckeridge and the second in

Cambridge, where I took myself to Caius and stood on the dark stairway outside the room that had been mine. From inside the room came the sound of soft, serious voices. It occurred to me that none in that room, however studious they might be, could know that the organ of the heart has no feeling.

On the third day I rode on towards Willingham and I saw how the landscape became, as it were, *less* and the sky *more* and how the creatures most numerous were the birds, who had their existence in both elements. A wind got up, making Danseuse nervous, so that she became for a while a dancer indeed, shying at gusts. But the birds rode on the wind. I watched them glide and plummet on the eddies. I saw bustards, and dottrels and wild geese.

And I observed how, in this Fen land, the crust of the earth appears thin, allowing water to seep and ooze upwards so that it is possible to imagine there are fishes and not worms in the soil. And it is a landscape of thin things – feathery marsh grasses and bullrushes and bending willows – so that I smiled when I thought of Pearce within it, thin and threadbare, and I also began to sense how I, with my wide, flat face, my fleshy lip and my soft belly, was not at one with it at all.

Though the wind seemed unable to cease (as if the vast cloudy sky held the wind trapped, as under a dome) no rain at all fell on me in all my journey and for this blessing I found myself giving thanks to the silent God of the lardy cake. And so in this way let my thoughts dwell upon the very simple credo that informs Pearce's life and which

makes him immune to all the spells under which I had
fallen. Despite much evidence to the contrary, he and his
Quaker friends believe that the Apostolic age is not over,
that God and his Son have much more to say to us yet, but
will not choose persons of worldly authority through
whom to say it. 'The Seed of Christ, Merivel,' Pearce had
informed me many times, 'is planted not in the souls of
Priests or Kings, but in the bosom of The Commonest
He,' thus causing whole hundreds of proud citizens to
quail with fear at the idea of God's word passing through
the likes of Cattlebury or the late Pierpoint and so to de-
nounce Quakerism as an utter heresy. Strangely, the King
(who does not appear to quail at anything, even death) is
tolerant towards Quakers – more tolerant of their dis-
courtesies than he has been towards mine. Were Pearce to
come into the King's presence and refuse to remove his
hat, I do not think he would have his house taken from
him. I could imagine, even, that the brazen gesture might
be rewarded with that gift I once held to be more priceless
than any other, the Royal Smile.

So, with my incoherent thoughts turning always in a
circular fashion back towards myself, I trotted on towards
the village of Doddington, and stayed my third night in
the little town called March, where I slept a most discon-
solate sleep, being full of trepidation about my imminent
arrival at Pearce's Hospital.

THE NEW BEDLAM, or Whittlesea Hospital, has been
founded in a place with the poetic name of Earls Bride, but

which I saw at once to be really no proper place at all, but a thin straggle of poor cottages, having no forge or ale house or dairy or any means that I could see of purchasing provisions. It is like a drowned place, a shipwrecked place. Those few who cling to it must endure a life of most fearful monotony, their only visitors being the birds and the buffeting wind. Upon my first sighting of Earls Bride (is there the ghost of a true bride in the name or has it corroded in the damp air, being once Bridle Way or even Bridge?) I had this most perverse thought: that the penning up of one hundred lunatics in their midst had brought some entertainment to the inhabitants of this Godforsaken place.

As we approached the Hospital, which is a cluster of barns built around a lime-washed low-roofed house such as might house a yeoman farmer, Danseuse stopped dead and, though I kicked vigorously at her flanks, she could not be persuaded forward. I dismounted and looked about me and listened. I could hear nothing except the huffing of the wind, but I note in passing that, since my meeting in the King's summer-house, my hearing seems to have suffered a most inexplicable loss, and I could tell from Danseuse's stubbornness and from the way her ears were pricked that she had heard a sound that made her uneasy.

Around the buildings has been constructed a flint and clay wall, like a bailey round a castle except that this structure was, I presumed, designed not to keep enemies out but to keep the mad folk in, lest they go roaming about in the flat land and drown. An iron gate had been let into the wall and it was towards this that I led Danseuse, having put a comforting arm round her neck.

The gate was locked. I knocked and waited and then turned and looked at desolate Earls Bride on its little causeway. It was the look of one who, suddenly feeble of spirit, wishes to turn round and retrace his steps homewards. And I know that, had Bidnold still been mine, I would have done this. I would not even have stayed to greet my old friend. I would, in short, have run away.

A tall man, large in every respect, with a great barrelled thorax and very mighty hands, opened the gate to me and stood smiling enquiringly. He had red curly hair, very thick and abundant, and a red beard, under which he made a steeple of his fingers.

'How may I help you, Friend?' he asked.

I nodded to him, the while noting a distressing shivering in the neck of my horse.

'I have come to see my friend, John Pearce and . . . well, in truth I really cannot say why else I find myself here, unless it is in the belief that I could be of some use . . .'

'Please enter. We will get oats for your horse. It is not a glad place you have come to, but a place of suffering. I expect you noticed our words from Isaiah upon the gate?'

'I saw some words, but did not read them.'

'Ah. Then read before you come in.'

The large man now returned his hand to the gate and pushed it to a little, as if making to shut me out. Had he closed it entirely, I do believe I would have turned my horse round and cantered away, but he did not.

I peered at the inscription beaten into the metal: 'Behold, I have refined thee but not with silver; I have chosen thee in the furnace of affliction' *Isaiah* 48.10.

'Very well,' I said. 'I have read the words.'

The gate moved again to admit me. I felt Danseuse's head push up against my restraining arm and she jangled her bit.

'Please follow me, Friend,' said the red-haired man who, I now noticed, was wearing a leather tabard over his black coat and leggings. The tabard was very stained and blackened with use, like a worn saddle. I looked down at my own clothes. I was wearing brown velvet breeches and a brown coat edged only a little with carmine. The lace at my wrists and throat was limp. My own good sense told me that, for all their relative modesty, these garments were not sturdy enough for the days that were coming.

I stepped inside, tugging my horse, and the gate closed behind us. We stood in a kind of courtyard with a floor of cinders, very patchy with moss. A single tree, an oak, grew in the middle of it.

'This,' said the man in the tabard, 'is the Airing Court. We believe in the healing property of air.'

'This is where they walk?'

'Yes. Round the tree and then round again, and so on, round and round, but the tree is not dull. It is a most restless and changeful tree. You see?'

'Yes. And now the spring is –'

'My name is Ambrose Dyer. I should have mentioned this at very first, for names are important with us.'

'I am glad to meet you, Mr Dyer.'

'And you?'

'I beg your pardon?'

'Your name?'

'Ah. Robert Merivel. Pearce and I were medical students together at Cambridge.'

'John. We do not call him Pearce. He is John. And I am Ambrose.'

'I believe, to me, he will always be Pearce. As he, in turn, addresses me as Merivel.'

'Here, he is John.'

'So I must be Robert?'

'And I am Ambrose. Now I shall name for you our buildings. The house itself we call Whittlesea House and this is where we, the founders and keepers, six in number have our rooms and where we eat together. And the three barns or *asiles*, meaning places of shelter, are called George Fox, and Margaret Fell, and William Harvey.'

Despite the trepidation I was feeling, I smiled to myself. Even here, in this lonely place with its one oak tree, Pearce had remembered his mentor, for of course it was true that he carried the great WH with him everywhere in his circulating blood.

'Which barn is called William Harvey?' I enquired.

'The smallest,' said Ambrose, 'to the left of us, here. Where those very deep into their madness are put.'

At that moment, as we walked towards the house, Pearce came out of it. When he looked up and saw me he appeared to gasp for air like a fish. And then, as I predicted he would, he broke into a stumbling run.

THAT NIGHT, I slept on Pearce's bed, with Pearce lying on a pallet on the floor not far from me. My mind seemed to inhabit a place much stranger than the room, so that I did not feel as if I slept but only fell in and out of odd, dreamlike trances. Each time I believed myself to be near to sleep I heard an echo of the King's voice, repeating the same words again and again: 'I have refined thee, Merivel. Behold, I have refined thee. But not with silver. Not with silver . . .'

A MONTH HAS passed. April has come. And it is as if, during this month, since my arrival at Whittlesea Hospital, I have been absent from myself. This morning, however, seeing my reflection in the parlour window I once again caught sight of him: the man you know all too well by this time; the person I asked you to picture wearing a scarlet suit; the Fool Merivel. And I could not prevent a sentimental tenderness towards Merivel from creeping over my skin, causing me to blush both with affection and with shame. It is this tenderness that has led me to continue the story, notwithstanding the dismaying fact that when I passed through the gates of the New Bedlam, I passed from one life into another and thus an ending of some kind has been reached. Under these things you may draw a line: my house at Bidnold, the colours of my park, Celia's face at my table. Neither you nor I will see them again. They have been consumed, not by actual flames, as were

my dear parents, but by the fire of the King's displeasure.
I must thus imagine them turned to ash, and so must you,
for you will not be returned to them.

I have become Robert.

No one at Whittlesea (not even Pearce, whom I must
address as John) calls me Merivel and many do not even
know that this is my name. I am not even Sir Robert. I am
Robert. And this is how you may picture me: I do not wear
my wig except at Meetings (these are most strange yet
moving things, which I will later describe), I go about my
work wearing black woollen breeches and a black woollen
shirt which causes a vexatious itching of my nipples.
These garments are covered by a leather apron, very
heavy, that comes down to my knees. My boots are low-
heeled and of sturdy hide and ever soiled with the mud of
Whittlesea, which is like no other mud I have seen, being
blackish and slimy and drying – when it does dry – to a
sulphurous yellow crust. My belly, grown very fat upon
Cattlebury's carbonados and syllabubs, is shrinking on
the poor diet of herring, frumenty, spoon-meat and water
favoured by Pearce and Ambrose and the other Quakers.
Even as a child, I was a mighty eater and the thinness of
the food on which I am here forced to live causes me a deal
of misery. Two pigeons are roosting in the poplar trees
outside the Bedlam gate and I would dearly love to see
their plump breasts roasted and set before me on a plate.
But such thoughts I set aside, as I must also set aside a
yearning (almost perpetual) to saddle Danseuse and ride
away from here. For where should I ride to? All paths,

outside this place, lead back to the King. This, at least, I have been permitted to understand. And so I remain, having no glimpse of any future.

I am allotted tasks, almost all of them of a menial and repellent variety and having some foul smell to them. But I perform them. The days I dread are those when I must work at William Harvey. Open the door of William Harvey and you are opening the door of hell. Yesterday, in William Harvey, a woman bit off the tip of her tongue even as I lifted her to put fresh straw into her pen and her blood spurted into my eyes and it was like a flame licking me and I felt a contamination of madness. The house is well named. There is an abundance of blood in it. There is blood in puddles on the floor.

There are many rules we must all obey at Whittlesea. One of these forbids any of the Keeping Friends (for so the small staff of the Bedlam quaintly call themselves) to go alone for any reason whether by day or by night into William Harvey. So it was that when the tip of the bitten tongue fell at my feet and I was splattered with blood, one Friend came quickly to my side. It was Eleanor who came, the younger of two sisters – Eleanor and Hannah – who are women of very sweet and sober disposition. She picked up the tongue tip and put it into her handkerchief and with admirable fortitude Pearce presently sewed it on again. But I prefer not to dwell upon that. I will, instead, tell you a little about these sisters and about the other Friends who make up this small company and who have under their care one hundred mad souls.

The Whittlesea Hospital was founded two years ago by Ambrose and Edmund. Its first occupant was Ambrose's grandfather, an old seaman who lost an eye to Spanish pirates and who, when the King returned, believed himself to have died. He lives quite happily in George Fox. He has an eye of glass that he keeps in a wooden box. He daily remarks that he expected the grave to be darker and more silent and is most glad that there should be company within it.

Ambrose, as noted at my first meeting with him at the gate, is large, obstinate, gentle and very hardy, like a plant with a great growth of root and an indifference to frost or heat or hail or drought. If all the world were to die of some epidemic, I do believe Ambrose would die last of all. Without him there would be no Whittlesea Hospital. Without him, Pearce would still be at St Barts in London and the others, Hannah and Eleanor, Edmund and Daniel, would still be waiting for the revelation of what they call 'the True Work shown to us through the Seed of Christ, which is in all people'.

Edmund is a man of my age who has twice been imprisoned for entering Anglican churches and causing harm to the clergy by the throwing of cabbages to their heads. He has most bright and round eyes and a high voice and is very fond of order and cleanliness, and will, when it rains in great sweeps across the Fens, take off all his clothes except a ragged pair of drawers and run round and round the walls, the while soaping his face and his torso and even his private parts. If Hannah or Eleanor should glance up and see Edmund engaged in these ablutions, I have noticed that they smile at each other and then look away and continue with their work, but that the smiles stay upon their faces for some while. It is as if they find, in Edmund's ritual, some innocent pleasure.

Both are large women with wide hips planted on sturdy legs. They wear sabots. Hannah's eyes are grey, Eleanor's blue. I believe Hannah to be thirty and Eleanor three or four years younger. They love the Lord with a great abundant love and their charity towards His creatures is very bountiful. I do not believe I have ever met any women like them, for they seem to have no vanity at all, but neither do they pity themselves, nor will let anyone speak their minds for them. In the month that has passed, I have once or twice prayed to be ill, so that Hannah and Eleanor might nurse me. But most strangely, given the unhealthy Fenland air and the inadequacy of my meals, I have not been ill one day. I content myself by sitting near them at supper, for I find their stillness comforting.

The sixth member of the Whittlesea staff is Daniel. He is the youngest of them all and his face has that transparent quality of youth – as if only time will give it proper substance. He is no more than seventeen. Having seen nothing of the world, nothing that he sees causes him any fright or revulsion. He is accepting of all things. He does not flinch from what he sees and smells and hears inside William Harvey. And of the six Friends, he is the most accepting of me. There is no disapproval in him. While the others wish to convert me to Quakerism, Daniel does not. Rather, being told that I was once at Court, he asks me to tell him in secret what that world of the Court is and how men speak and how they dress and what things they devise as pastimes. So I find myself describing the game of croquet, and Daniel listens and repeats such explanations as 'Red may now, having passed under the hoop, endeavour to roquet Black' with reverence, as if they were the Twenty-third Psalm. And the two of us are momentarily very happy until I remember that I no longer have any rightful place in the world where croquet is played and so would do best to forget its complicated rules. And so I break off and Daniel is, for a mere moment or two, cast down. 'Why might we not,' he asked me one day, 'play a little croquet here, Robert?' I pretend to give this some thought before answering: 'The sight of a croquet hoop would make John most unhappy, Daniel.'

And so I come to 'John', as I must now call my spindly friend, Pearce.

The joy and surprise with which he greeted me were soon enough superceded by a return to the severity with which he always feels obliged to treat me. As I expected, he was neither surprised by my fall from Royal grace nor sympathetic towards my distress.

'When I saw what your life was, in that terrible luxurious house of yours,' he said, 'I prayed you would be taken out of it.'

'Yet I, Pearce, was uncommonly fond of it,' I felt obliged to remind him.

'John,' he said.

'What, Pearce?'

'Call me John, if you will.'

'I am bound, after all this time, to find that difficult.'

'You find difficult *all* that is simple and good, Robert. That is the trouble with you.'

This conversation took place in Pearce's room late on the night of my arrival at Whittlesea, I resting my wind-buffeted body on his narrow bed, he lying on a pallet (such as is used by the occupants of George Fox and Margaret Fell) on the floor. I looked at him – my friend and my refuge! He is thinner than ever he was, so that the bones of his wrists resemble ivory bobbins. He is suffering, here in this low-lying land, from a very thick catarrh which causes bubbles of spittle to keep bursting at the corners of his mouth and which has quite silted up his sinuses, so that his voice sounds as if it was issuing from his nose. For this catarrh, he is dosing himself with mithridate which, in turn, has inflamed his eyes. He is, all in all, a wretched sight.

Though Quakers are not fond of sermons, Pearce lying on a straw mattress and dribbling mithridate into his nostrils, earnestly delivered himself of a sermon upon the perfidy of the Stuart Kings. 'None of them were,' he said, 'nor none will ever be worthy of the nation's trust. For the good of the nation is never first with them. What is first is their supposed Divinity that puts them outside or above the law, so that in all their actions they are accountable to no one, neither in their public nor their private life . . .'

While listening to this sermon, I found myself pondering not the truth or otherwise of Pearce's words, but my own absence of anger in the whole disastrous matter.

Wounded, disappointed, afraid, melancholy: these I am. What I do not seem to be is angry. So, refraining from agreeing or disagreeing with Pearce's diatribe against the Stuarts, I simply burst out: 'Why do I not feel angry, Pearce?'

'John.'

'John. Why do I not feel angry, John?'

'Because you are a child.'

'I beg your pardon?'

'A child, punished by selfish parents, does not feel anger. It goes to its little private corner to weep. Exactly as you have done. And if the parents should again hold out their arms, why then the child will come running into them, all glad to be returned and forgiven for something it did only in answer to their greed.'

'But Pearce –'

'Just as, if the King were to call you back, you would go running!'

'He will not call me back. It is quite finished.'

'No. But were he to do so, you would go. And this is how it is revealed to me that you are still a child, Robert. But, mercifully for you, your state of homelessness brought you to Whittlesea. Our task here is to cure you of childishness just as we are trying to cure the lunatics of their insanity. For the man in you could be most splendid, Robert. I saw the shaping of the man – before you reverted to being the child – and it is that man we shall restore to you.'

I glanced down at Pearce. I noticed that by him on the

floor, within reach of his cadaverous fingers, he had placed
his precious soup ladle. And I smiled.

AFTER THAT FIRST night, I found that Pearce was not
interested in discussing my past life or my loss of it. He
wished me to put it out of my mind as speedily as possible
and so from the following day (during which I was given
the drab clothes I have described for you) I was expected
to join in the work of the Keepers exactly as if I were one
of them and a born Quaker. 'Robert is well qualified to
help us,' Pearce announced to Ambrose, Edmund, Hannah, Eleanor and Daniel over our dawn breakfast of barley
and water porridge. 'He is not squeamish or frail. He
claims to have forgotten medicine, but I know that he has
not. So let us give thanks to Christ that He has sent Robert to us and ask Him to sustain him in the work we shall
find for him to do.'

There followed prayers of touching simplicity. 'Lord,
send a light to show Robert the way,' said Ambrose. 'Dear
Jesus, be with Robert,' said Eleanor. 'God in Heaven, take
Robert's hand and be at his side,' said Hannah. 'And even
when night comes, still be at his side,' said Daniel. 'Amen,'
said Edmund.

I look round at the little company. Alas, I think, they do
not know me. I am John's friend, and he has vouched for
me and so they have taken me in. But they do not know
how afraid I am. They do not know that I have long been
parted from God. They do not know there is a madness in
me which renders grass and trees as lunatic lines and

splodges. They have taken me in to Bedlam, but they do not know that my spirit rejoices in chaos. I am wrong for them and I will do them wrong, and they do not know it. I opened my mouth to begin upon telling them what kind of man I was, but no words came to me except mumbled words of thanks for their prayers, 'for which,' I told them, 'I hope to make myself worthy.' And I saw Pearce nod approvingly at my sudden humility.

The broken silence

I DID NOT know that on the evening of the twenty-first of April I was going to break my silence at the Meetings. Though very fascinated by the 'truth' I had stumbled upon about the world's inability to try any cure upon the lunatic until he is – in all but a few cases – incurable, I had not planned to offer any discourse upon the subject until I had pondered what practical measures might be taken to remedy this situation. Still less had I plotted within myself to reveal to the Keepers my all-too-Merivelian ideas about the efficacy of weeping and sweating in the treatment of poisonous humours.

And yet, all these things came out of me. And the manner of their coming out was most memorable and strange.

I was seated at one edge of the little semi-circle we make at Meetings round the parlour fire. Near me, on an oak table, was a wooden bowl into which Pearce had put posies of primroses. There was utter silence in the room except for the crackling and spitting of the fire, and there is something about a Quaker silence which is absolute, as if Eternity were then and there beginning.

And in this quiet, I heard myself breathing in the smell of the flowers and after some minutes a certainty stole upon me that this perfume was slowly, with each breath of it that I took, being drawn up into my brain and there being alchemised into syllables and words. And it was not long before my brain seemed to be so full of words – as crammed with them as was the bowl with the primroses – that it began to hurt, and I put my head in my hands to try to get the hurt away. But it would not go. And so I opened my mouth and I began to speak, starting with the phrase, 'It has come to me from the Lord,' and in a perfectly logical fashion I set forth my argument, saying that madness may be born of many things but yet for all except those who are lunatic from their births there was a Time Before, a time when there was no madness in them and that this would be followed by a Growing Time or a Sickening Time, when the madness was coming upon them, precisely as all disease has a Growing Time. 'And we,' I said, 'we the Keepers of those who are very far gone into a mad sickness, do we not all recognise that the men and women of William Harvey are much further from any help or cure than those in the other two houses? Likewise, is it not our daily fear to find an inhabitant of George Fox or Margaret Fell descended into an uncontrollable mad state, so that we would be forced to chain him up and put him in a pen in William Harvey? Thus we daily admit that madness is not a static thing but, just as all things in the world are changeful, so is madness and, like them, may change for the better or for the worse. But what we do not ask, dear Friends, is what were the Footsteps of each case of madness, in other words how it came there and when and in what manner it first showed itself, yet I, when I was a physician, was taught by the great medical minds of our age that few cures are likely to succeed unless each stage and symptom of a malady is understood. And this is what the Lord has revealed to me, that we should try with each one of those in our care to look back into past time and ask them to try to remember how it was to be in the Time Before and what thing or calamity came about to put them into the Sickening Time. And in this way we might discover the imprint of the steps to madness, there just under the surface, as the imprints of past ages lie under the surface of the earth . . .'

As I delivered myself of this long speech, I was not aware of how the others regarded it or me, but only of my need to get it out so that my brain would be free of it and no longer hurting in the press of words. I deliberately paused at this point and took in several great breaths and once more the scent of the primroses ascended to my brain and recommenced its alchemy and so I talked on, now making proposals, all of which, I said, had 'come to me from Jesus Christ', for the questioning of all inmates of Whittlesea by the Keepers so that the Time Before might become visible to us. And I was entirely held now by my words, as if my words had become a liquid and I immersed in them, like a drowning man in a rushing river. So into the stream now poured all my outlandish things, my fantastical things, my cures by weeping and my cures by dancing, my suggestions for story-telling and the playing of music. As I spoke on these matters, I began to feel a merciful diminution of the pain in my head and so I lifted it up and talked on, staring at the fire, and in the flames of the fire I could see a most wondrous picture of Daniel, attired in the clothes of summer, playing a fiddle, and all the women of Margaret Fell skipping and dancing round him, seeming happy like children. And then the pain left me entirely and the picture vanished and I was silent.

I was very boiling hot. I took off my wig and wiped my face and my head with my handkerchief. I felt the eyes of the others upon me, but no one spoke. A full ten or fifteen minutes passed and the time allowed for the Meeting came to an end and Ambrose put his hands into his prayer steeple and mumbled: 'Thank you, dear Lord, that in our presence Robert was moved to speak.' And this is all that was said.

MERCIFULLY, IT WAS not my turn that night to take part in a Night Keeping, for as soon as we rose from our circle by the fire, I felt a shivering in my knees and a pain of exhaustion in my belly and I went to my bed and slept a deep, thick sleep from which I did not stir till morning.

When I woke, however, I felt in me a lightness of heart, such as I had not experienced since my casting out from Bidnold. I could not account for it, but was most grateful to find it there. (I have, since I arrived here, found myself pondering the thing we call happiness, for which the King once told me I had a gift. I now recognise that my supposed 'gift' was much less of a thing than, say, Hannah's and Eleanor's, they being two of the most contented women I have ever met.)

It was my task, that morning, to work in the vegetable garden with Pearce, together with some six or seven men from George Fox. (I report in passing that Pearce is so fond of this plot, so proud of its drainage ditches and of the infant pear trees he is trying to grow *en espalier* on its southerly wall, that he likes to oversee all work done there and becomes very vaporous with irritation if his seedlings are not planted in absolutely straight lines.) The sun was once again shining and I would have found my duty in the garden quite pleasant had it not been for Pearce's behaviour towards me that morning, which was most irksome. He acted as one who wished to have nothing to do with me whatsoever, separating himself from any task in which I was occupied and replying most curtly to all my attempts to speak to him. Watching him from a distance planting beans, swooping down on a freshly raked patch of soil like a long-necked bird, using his long white fingers as a dibbling-stick, burying each bean most lovingly and moving on, I remembered how on our angling expeditions near Cambridge this mood of dislike for me would sometimes come over him. Then and now, I find it most hurtful and difficult to endure, particularly as I can seldom fathom what it is I have done to offend him. On this morning, however, I could only conclude that my outpouring of the previous evening had not been to his liking. Some hours – or even days – would probably pass; then Pearce would dissect my thesis with his clever pecking mind and lay it in ruins before me.

Meanwhile, as I plucked weeds from the onion bed, I began in a low voice, lest Pearce hear what I was doing, to talk to the man called Jacob Lowe who was working alongside me and to enquire of him what thing he most clearly remembered before coming to Whittlesea and whether, in his past life, he had some trade or calling. He told me he was a butcher and slaughterer. He described to me the ease with which he could split a calf's head and take out the tender brains. 'But I was killed by a whore,' he whispered. 'I died of her foul cunt. And this is my second life on earth.'

I requested him to describe his 'death' to me. And he told me that his testicles had swollen and burst 'being full of the pox' and out through these burst cods had poured his life.

I looked up at Jacob Lowe. His face was ruddy, his musculature good, his nose prominent and not one whit decayed. From these external signs, I felt it possible to conclude that, if he had once suffered from the pox, he was now cured of it. Such cures are rare but where they occur they have depended – in all cases I have witnessed – on the giving of *mecurius sublimate*, of which the chief element is mercury itself, that capricious metal to which I once likened the King. And mercury is, if the dose is not most carefully measured, a poison. I saw a man at St Thomas's die of mercury poisoning and he died screaming and raving, as if a madness had suddenly come upon him. I smiled to myself and looked over to Pearce's stooping back. In the time it had taken me and Jacob Lowe to weed the onion patch, I had retraced the primary footsteps to this one man's lunacy.

Neither at dinnertime nor during the afternoon did any of the friends make reference to my speech of the evening before and Pearce's lack of charity towards me seemed to confirm that he at least had been most displeased by it. I thus kept quiet to myself my conversation with Jacob Lowe and waited for the Meeting to see if Ambrose might pass judgement upon my theory. But he did not mention it, and I confess I felt somewhat cast down to think that what had appeared to me as a revelation appeared to the Keepers of Whittlesea as a thing of no consequence at all. It was only some days later that I was to discover that their way with knowledge is a quiet way. They do not snatch at it or gobble it down; they take it into themselves slowly like a physic and let it course a long time in their blood before making any pronouncement upon it.

Meanwhile, Pearce emerged from his state of foulness towards me and bade me go with him one morning in search of yet more flowers. Not far from the Whittlesea gate we came upon some pale, sweet-scented narcissus, which Pearce instructed me to pick.

'You see,' he said, as I gathered the flowers for him, 'I am in a most troubling state of unknowing, Robert.'

'Are you, John?' I said.

'Yes. For I vowed that in this springtime I would find an answer to a question that has vexed me for many years, namely, what is the scent of flowers? Why is it there? Do plants exhale? Is the scent no more than this exhaled breath? And if there is no exhalation, then in what part of a flower resides the scent?'

'Why do you wish to know this, John?' I enquired.

'*Why*? Because I do *not* know it. There is undoubtedly some Divine lesson hidden in the mystery, but until I have unravelled the mystery itself, I am shut out from knowing what it might be.'

I held out my bunch of narcissus to Pearce and he took it delicately from me, like a girl. I was tempted to say that the smell of the primroses had led me to knowledge I believed more useful than any he might derive from the study of flowers, but I did not.

Branches of pear

I BADE GOODNIGHT to all the Keepers. I went to my linen cupboard and lit my lamp and I took this with me to Pearce's room, so that we had two lamps by which to work. I also took with me my surgical instruments, cleaned meticulously these days, with their silver handles polished.

As Pearce sat down on his narrow bed, I said: 'I'll wager you have caught a summer chill and this is all.'

'No,' said Pearce, 'I have had chills before and this is not one.'

'Well, let us see . . .'

I began by taking up a tongue depressor and looking down Pearce's throat, which did not appear inflamed though I noted that his tongue was a little swollen and coated and that his breath was foul. I then examined his neck for swellings and found none. Then, guided by his hand, I put my hand on that part of his head that felt cold to him and through his thinning hair felt it to be moist, as if there was a sweating there.

This done, I asked him to take off his coat and shirt and to lie down on his bed, so that I could listen to his heart-beat and his breathing.

While he undressed, I made notes about the strange moistness of his head, the cause of which I could not at first fathom. Then I looked up.

Pearce stood before me, folding his shirt into a bundle, wearing only his frayed black breeches and stockings. I thought back to the last time I had seen his arms and chest unclothed, which was during my vigil at his bedside in the Olive Room at Bidnold. He had been as thin then as he always was as a young man, but now the change in his appearance was distressing beyond words to behold, for he was like a veritable skeleton, with his chest quite concave and every rib visible to me, seeming to have no covering of soft warm flesh on him at all, rather his bones appearing held together by his white skin.

'Pearce . . .' I stammered, forgetting in my shock at the sight of him, his constant entreaty to me to call him John.

'Yes,' he said, 'I know. I am grown a little thin.'

'A little!' I blurted out. 'What has happened to you? Have you been fasting?'

'No, I eat what is put before me. I do not know how this weight has been lost.'

'Lie down!' I snapped.

Obediently, Pearce set aside his bundle and lay on his back on his bed. I brought the two lamps as near to him as I could and looked down at him and, truly, I wanted to cuff him about his head for allowing his body, invisible to us all inside his baggy clothes, to waste away to this degree.

I took up his wrist and felt his pulse and was relieved to find it quite strong. Then I bent over him and put my head on his chest and heard his heartbeat against my ear.

'It is the lung you should be listening to,' said Pearce.

'I know,' I said crossly. 'Inhale deeply and exhale as slowly as you can.'

The intake of breath was not smooth. It had a kind of spasm to it, as if there was a sobbing in the body.

'Inhale again and keep on with slow breaths until I tell you to stop,' I instructed.

I listened for several minutes, moving my listening position a little after every second breath, then I told Pearce to turn over and I put my ear to his back, which is a most wretched part of the man, being very scabby with pimples, and all of what I heard made me afraid, for I was in no doubt that the lungs were in distress, having in them a quantity of mucus or phlegm which, if it is not got out, will in time fill all the lung tissue and bring the sufferer to a cruel death like a slow drowning.

'It is a poisonous congestion, is it not?' said Pearce, sitting up and rubbing his eyes, which I now saw were very heavy with tiredness.

'Yes,' I said.

'And the sweating and coldness in my head?'

'Probably a beneficial evacuation. A means by which the matter is endeavouring to come out.'

'And if it does not come out?'

'We will bring it out. But you must rest, Pearce.'

'John.'

'John, then! But you will be neither one nor the other and no name will matter one whit, if you allow yourself to die!'

'I cannot stay in my bed, Robert, when there is so much work to do here.'

'You must stay in your bed, or the remedies I shall prescribe will have no help from you, only hindrance.'

'No, I cannot. For we must reveal nothing of this to Ambrose or the others.'

'Pearce,' I said crossly, 'please do not make me lose my patience! Have I not, a hundred times since we met at Caius, allowed you to command me and let you be wise and done this or that thing at your bidding? I *have*! So do not even consider contradicting me on this score. For I am determined you will do this one thing that I am ordering you to do, and that is to stay here in your bed and let us care for you and not to stir from this room till you are well. And if you do not do this, John, you will no longer be my friend or any true Friend to Whittlesea. You will be in your grave!'

Pearce then allowed his head to fall back on his pillow and he nodded. 'Very well,' he said, 'but only for a little time. What will you prescribe?'

'Syrup of roses to warm your blood and soothe your coughing. A burdock poultice or a bread poultice for your head.'

'And for the slime in the lung?'

'Sal Ammoniac.'

'And a balsam?'

'Yes. We shall try several, dissolved in boiling water and inhaled.'

'Good. It has all returned to you then, Robert?'

'What has returned?'

'The right knowledge for the right time.'

'Perhaps.'

'As of course it had to. For we can never truly unknow what we have known or unsee what we have seen, can we?'

'Probably not, John,' I said. 'Now please do me the favour of taking off your breeches and putting on your nightshirt.'

* * *

TWO WEEKS PASSED, during which I wished to turn all my thoughts and all my strength to the cures I was trying upon Pearce. But they were weeks in which I found myself subjected to a great clamouring from the people of George Fox and Margaret Fell who, whenever I went among them, begged me to let them come out and dance once again, informing me that dancing was the only cure for them and that all their madness was caused in the first place by the absence of music.

I laid the problem before the Keepers, but none had any solution. That the tarantella had had some beneficial effect on those allowed out that afternoon seemed certain; what was also certain was that, in those we had kept chained up, the music and clapping and shrieking had engendered feelings of rage and despair that took many days to subside.

Suggestions were made. Edmund declared it might be feasible to chain the inhabitants of WH one to another and lead them out across the Earls Bride causeway, out of earshot of the music. Hannah ventured that we could give them opiates to drug them to sleep. But we held back from approving either of these ideas, the reason being that both of them made us feel uneasy.

And so the clamour for the dancing went on and with it a clamour of another kind, which was from Katharine, who truly believed herself in love with me and I could not approach her without she entreated me to touch her. The sight of her black hair, her strong legs and her full breasts began to occupy my mind to such a horrible degree that even as I sat at Pearce's bed-side and covered his head, while he inhaled my balsam preparations, or I laid poultices on his crown, I would feel this clamour of Katharine in my body and I would grow hot and sometimes breathless and sick in my stom-ach. Then, silently, I would curse the day I had taken pity on her, and feel scorn for myself in the realisation that even in this action I had been moved by words once spoken to me by the King, so that even at Whittlesea – far, as I thought, beyond his reach – I was not yet entirely free of him.

Several visitors to Whittlesea were turned away by us during this time, our fear of bringing in the plague still being very great. One of these visitor's was Katharine's mother. She had brought her daughter a honeycomb and a pair of green slippers with some fine embroidery on them. When Ambrose informed her that she could not come in, she grew very angry and declared that all who care for the mad and the sick, though they pretend to be charitable people, are the greatest deceivers of the age, their only aim being to line their own pockets. She walked away still cursing Ambrose so violently that she, too, appeared to be touched with madness.

Eleanor gave the honeycomb and the green slippers to Katharine. When she knew that her mother had been turned away, Katharine began to cry. She told Eleanor that a cure for her condition existed in the world but that we were all too blind to see what it was.

* * *

JULY CAME IN and, in this month, three things of importance took place.

The first of these things was the arrival of another letter from Will Gates, informing me that my horse, Danseuse, had walked in through the park gates at Bidnold 'a little lame in her left hind leg and with no bridle on her, but only a saddle, twisted round'. Will asked me to write to him, to tell him I was alive. 'If you are alive, Sir,' said the letter, 'I will continue to keep and hide your horse from the V. de Confolens, so that you can get her for you again. But if, as I fear, you are dead, I will send W. Jossett, your groom, with her to the King, so that His Majesty can know of your sad end.'

This letter, if I had not been so very preoccupied by the condition of Pearce and by the behaviour of Katharine, would have gladdened my spirits a great deal, not only because it made me laugh, but also because the news of Danseuse's return seemed to me miraculous and therefore to portend some good. As it was, there did not seem to be adequate space in my mind for the tidings that it contained.

Keeping an afternoon vigil by Pearce's bed, while he slept his snarling invalid's sleep, I wrote a short letter thanking Will and enclosing money to buy oats for my horse. 'I do not know,' I said in this letter, 'how or if ever I shall come again to Bidnold, so if I have not come there in the space of one year from now, please return Danseuse to His Majesty the King and say that I am no longer in the world.'

The second thing of importance was the beginning of a recovery in Pearce. I confess I felt not only relieved that my friend seemed to be retreating from a premature encounter with death, but also gratified that *my* syrups and balsams, *my* insistence upon rest and good nourishment (I had devised for Pearce a very good diet of coddled eggs, boiled meat, chicory and malted bread), were the means by which he seemed to be returning to health. When I listened to his breathing now, I could still hear a wheezing in the lungs, but the balsams and the Sal Ammoniac had helped him cough up a great quantity of phlegm from them and the burdock poultices had turned the moist patch on his crown to a dribbling sore, from which much foul matter was able to come out.

After three weeks, in which he slept every afternoon and was content to let us bring him his meals and to wash him and comb his sparse hair and generally care for him like an infant, he began to protest that he was cured and ready to resume what he called his 'proper task, which is not the comforting of myself, but the comforting of others'. So we let him get up and helped him to put on his clothes that were still very much too large for his thin body, despite the eggs and the malted loaves, and he came downstairs and went out into the sunshine and asked me to walk with him to the vegetable garden so that he could see his pear trees.

It is a feature of Pearce's character, as I think I may already have told you, that he believes himself to be the only person upon earth capable of carrying out certain tasks, one of which is the cultivation of fruit trees *en espalier*. It was thus that he expected, after three weeks' absence from them, to find his trees dead and shrivelled, and when he saw that they were not, despite the great heat of the last month, he assumed at once that it was God who had saved them and he knelt down in the vegetable garden and gave up thanks to his Maker when, in reality, he should have given up thanks to me and to Edmund who had spent many tedious hours watering the wretched trees, aware as we were of Pearce's wrath and sadness if we should let them die. I was tempted to inform him of this, but I did not. I stood and watched him praying and I knew that, as always, my irritation with him would not last, it being so diluted by my affection for him that it is like a single drop of aloes in a jug of mead. So, instead of reproaching Pearce, I, too, found myself conversing with God, who seems nearer to me here than He ever seemed at Bidnold. I asked Him to bring my old friend back to perfect health and I added: 'I will remember to call him John, Lord, if you will remember to put some flesh on his bones.'

And so to the third event of this month of July which, of all the things that have happened since I came to Whittlesea, is the worst thing, for now it haunts me continuously and I know that the shame it brings upon me is so great that were the Keepers to know of it, I would be sent out from here – my long friendship with Pearce notwithstanding – and ordered never to return.

It took place on a hot night which seems to have been

so short, it was as if there was no darkness at all, but only a fading of the sky and then a lightening of it again.

I woke not long after midnight, having slept for only a few minutes. I felt full of trouble and fearful dreaming. Every part of me was sweating and filled with such an aching discomfort that I knew I could not lie another minute in my bed.

I stood up and looked out of my window and all that my eye would light upon in this particular pale midnight was the door of Margaret Fell and I knew that my struggle against my lust for Katharine was lost.

I put on a thin shirt and some breeches and then I let myself quietly out of my room and paused and listened in case any of the Keepers was stirring, but the house was silent except for the sound of Pearce's snoring.

Once out in the night air and feeling its sweetness upon my face, all fear of what I was about to do left me, so that I did not go to it with trepidation, as I should have done, but with a false joy, pretending to myself that it was an honourable thing and a thing that would bring peace and rest.

I opened the door of Margaret Fell and went in, closing it behind me. I did not move, but stood in the darkness until I could see the two rows of sleeping women. I looked over to where Katharine lay with her doll and her green embroidered slippers that she now also cradled to her and to which she sometimes spoke, as if to a child.

She was sitting up and looking over to where I stood. I did not go to her. I waited. She put down the slipper she had been holding and got up and came towards me. I saw the woman lying next to Katharine wake up and stare at her and then at me, but I paid this other person no heed at all.

As Katharine came close to me, I reached out for her with my left hand and with my right hand I opened the door to the operating room of Margaret Fell where only a short while ago I had helped perform an autopsy and wrapped a dead woman in her winding sheet.

The floor of this room is stone and on this stone I knelt down and pulled Katharine down by me and kissed her mouth and then her breasts. And both of us tore from the other our clothes, being very full of greed and readiness. And naked together we crawled into the dark space under the operating table. And there, it seemed, Katharine imagined herself once again above the vaults of a church, for she began to whisper to me that at last we were together in God's house. And though God may never forgive me for this, I confess I was excited by this blasphemy, and I did with Katharine in the space of an hour everything she asked of me and more that my own mind could devise. And this was no simple Act of Oblivion, but a love of the most Profane kind.

THIS NIGHT BEGAN what I now call my Time of Madness at Whittlesea.

There had been a Time Before. In the Time Before, as I have shown you, I believed that all my dealings with the Keepers and with the inmates were true and honest. I did not dissemble. I took out my lost skills from the darkness to which I had consigned them and laid them at the service of the community. I had been renamed and I strove to become worthy of that name. And if the old Merivel sometimes reappeared, sighing over his lost past, he also tried to make himself useful, as on the afternoon of the tarantella. As Pearce said of my oboe playing, it was evident to all that I was 'making progress'.

That 'progress' could not continue after I entered the operating room of Margaret Fell with Katharine, for from that moment I became addicted to my own foulness so entirely that my mind, instead of contemplating the work of each day, was filled up with it and I entered willingly on the most terrible deceptions just to come to it again.

When I woke, on the morning after that first night, and remembered what I had done, I felt mortally afraid. I knelt down by my bed and confessed to God: 'I have suffered a contamination of madness and now I am unclean and full of the Devil, but I will not do those things again, if you will help to drive the Devil from me!'

When I went down to breakfast in the kitchen, Hannah remarked that I looked pale, and I admitted to the Friends that I did not feel well that morning, it proving very difficult for me to swallow the porridge set before me, or even to hold my spoon because of a trembling in my hands.

I did not shun the work of the day, however, which included an airing for the inhabitants of William Harvey – always a most difficult and lengthy task, for before they can be brought out into the air all of them must be washed, some of their own excrement. And as the day progressed, the fear and shame by which I had been overcome upon waking gradually went from me and were replaced by a most acute longing to go into Margaret Fell and seize Katharine roughly by the hand and push her before me into the dark room and begin again on the shameless acts I had promised that morning to renounce.

And so began the pattern of each day during the Time of Madness: each morning, I vowed I would never, as long as I lived, touch Katharine again nor let her hand seek me out; each night, I lay and waited without sleeping for the moment when I could slip out into the darkness and go to find her.

It was soon known by the other inhabitants of Margaret Fell what kind of acts we performed in the operating room and the women would sometimes cluster by the door, listening, and when we came out some of them would claw at me, at my mouth and at my sex, and beg me to take them also. And this longing that they had and their knowledge of what I was doing made me feel very sick and afraid, for I knew that sooner or later some behaviour or word of theirs would betray me to the Keepers and I would be sent away. I was deceiving Pearce (perhaps for the first time in my life, for I had never before pretended to him that I was leading an honest life when I was not) and I was deceiving Ambrose and the others, who had taken me in and tried to make me one of them. But more terrible, perhaps, than either of these deceptions was my deceiving of Katharine who, finding herself in love with me, asked me to swear that I was in love with her and that, if the day came for me to leave Whittlesea, I would take her with me. And so I swore. But the truth was that I did not love her at all. Pity had drawn me to her, and my own lust, suddenly a most overpowering and demented thing, kept me there with her in the darkness. And when I asked myself whether, in time, I would grow to love her, I knew the answer: the possibility of my growing to love Katharine was as remote as the possibility of Celia growing to love me.

I HAD GONE on, undiscovered in the Time of Madness, for about five weeks when, returning one night to my room near one o'clock, I heard a voice call out, 'Merivel!'

I stood on the landing, shivering a little, certain that Robert had been found out at last and was being summoned as Merivel to be given his punishment. I waited and the voice called again, 'Merivel!' And then I recognised it as Pearce's voice and I moved slowly towards his room.

I opened the door. He had lit a rushlight by his bed and was lying on his side with his face very near the taper and he held one of his thin hands out towards me, palm upwards, in the gesture of a beggar.

'John,' I said, 'what do you want?'

'Merivel . . .' he said again, and his voice sounded thick with his old catarrh, 'I was waiting for you . . .'

'Waiting for me?'

'To come in. I heard you go out and I waited for you to return, so that I could call you and not wake the others.'

'Yes,' I said. 'I go and walk in the air sometimes at night, if I cannot sleep . . .'

'I heard you.'

I went nearer to Pearce. I know him so well that I can discern anger on his lips before he has uttered a word and I looked hard at him to see if it was there or not. It was not there, and the relief I felt was very great. What I could see, however, as I approached his bed, was that his face was running with sweat and that his cheeks (usually of such translucent whiteness it is difficult to believe that Pearce spends any of his time in the open air, let alone a great part of his day hoeing and pruning in his vegetable garden) had a hectic bright redness to them, the two things announcing to me at once that he had a high fever.

I went to him and laid my hand on his forehead. My hand burned.

'John . . .' I began.

'Yes. Very well. There is some fever. I was about to tell you that. I did not call you to repeat to me something I already know.'

'Why did you call me, then?'

'I called you because . . .'

'What?'

'I cannot find my ladle. I think it has fallen and rolled under the bed.'

I knelt down and felt about in the dust under his wooden bed, but could not discover it. I moved round and round the bed, searching under it as far as my arm would reach, but the thing was not there.

'I cannot see it, John.'

'Please find it, Merivel.'

'Why do you call me "Merivel"?'

'Did I call you that?'

'Yes.'

'When in truth you are . . . who? I cannot for just this one moment remember your other name.'

'Robert.'

'Robert?'

'Yes.'

'And yet tonight, since this fever began . . . that name Robert seems to have slipped away from my mind and what I remember is Merivel and how we once together witnessed a very miraculous thing and that was a visible beating heart. Do you recall that?'

'Yes, I do, John.'

'And you, because I could not, put your hand in and touched it.'

'Yes.'

'Yet the man felt nothing.'

'He felt nothing.'

'So pray for me, that I might become that person.'

'Why?'

'To feel no pain in my heart or anywhere.'

'Are you in pain?'

'Have you found the ladle?'

'No. It does not seem to be under the bed.'

'Please try to find it.'

'I do not know where else to look. Where shall I look?'

'Ssh. Don't raise your voice. You will wake the others.'

'I shall wake the others unless you tell me about the pain. Is it the pain you had before, in the lung?'

'Could anyone have stolen my ladle?'

'No. And I will find it for you. Where is the pain, John? Show me or tell me. Where is it?'

Pearce looked up at me. His faded blue eyes, in this dim rushlight, looked a darker colour than they were. He withdrew his hand and placed it, in a hesitant way, against his chest.

I stood up. I told him I refused to continue my search for the ladle until I had listened to his breathing. Then I gently helped him to turn onto his back and folded back the bedclothes and laid my head (which a mere half hour ago Katharine had taken in her hands and forced to suckle her breast like a baby) first on his sternum and then lower on his diaphragm.

I found Pearce's ladle under his pillows and handed it to him. I told him I was going to boil water for a balsam inhalation, then I left him for a while and went to my room and washed myself, for the smell of Katharine seemed to cling to every part of me. I put on a clean nightshirt and combed my hair. Only then did I go down to the kitchen and begin to prepare the only remedies I and all the world of medical science could offer for my friend's condition, knowing as I worked that this time they would not be strong enough to make him well.

* * *

WHAT I BEGAN that night and what we, the Keepers of Whittlesea, continued between us for ten days and nights was a constant vigil at Pearce's bedside.

On the fifth or sixth day, the pain of his breathing became so great for him that he whispered to me: 'I would not have imagined longing, as ardently as I do, for my last breath.'

We gave him opiates and as these entered his blood (there to be circulated to every part of him, as proved by his beloved mentor, WH) he seemed to fall, not into a sleep, but into a kind of dream of the past, so that he babbled to us of his mother who had been a widow for twenty years and who said prayers every day of her life for the soul of her dead husband, a barber, who had left her nothing but the tools of his trade with which, as soon as her son had been accepted into Caius College, she cut her own throat. She was buried not in the churchyard beside her husband, but 'at a crossroads, distant from the village; a place where people on foot or on horse-back or in carriages went this way or that, but did not stop'. He told us how, if we opened his Bible at Matthew, Chapter Ten, we would find 'the imprint of a bird across the writing'. He said he could not remember what species of bird it was, only that it was small and that he had found it 'freshly dead when I was a child and my mother still living'. He seemed very anxious that we should see this imprint, so I took up his Bible and searched for it and found eventually – not in Matthew, but across two pages of Mark – a brown greasy smudge, such as might have been made by the accidental placing on the Holy Book of a hot cinnamon pancake. I showed it to Pearce. 'Is this it, John?' I asked. He stared at it, his dilated pupils having difficulty focusing upon it. 'Yes,' he said at last. 'The viscera were removed, for I did not want to pollute the words of Jesus. And then I laid the bird in and opened out the wings and closed the book and put weights upon it and pressed it like a flower.'

I looked up at Hannah, who sat on the other side of Pearce's bed, bathing his brow from time to time with lavender water. She shook her head, showing me that she did not think this story about the pressed bird could be true, both of us being obliged to imagine the stench of the dead creature as it decayed in its tomb of sacred words. Had Pearce been well, I would have made the observation that the scent of death in a vertebrate does not resemble at all the scent of death in a flower, but, very far from being well, Pearce was by this time so weak that he could barely raise his head from the pillow, onto which what remained of his thin hair was gradually falling out.

The knowledge that Pearce was going to die was, during those ten days, like something draped round me, something that I *wore* but refused to take into my mind. And I do not think that this refusal was based upon any false hope that Ambrose or I could save him. What I had understood, I believe, is that no amount of knowing in advance that I was going to lose my friend could adequately prepare me for the actual loss of him when it came.

* * *

ON THE SEVENTH or eighth day of Pearce's sickness, both the pain in his lungs and his fever diminished for a while. He asked me to lift him up and prop him with cushions 'but not any with tassels or jewels on them or any gaudy ones such as you had in your house'. I smiled. I put my hands gently into his armpits (where there seems to be no flesh any more, only a webbing of skin) and pulled him towards me while Daniel set some pillows at his back. I asked him if he would try to eat a little broth. He said he would and Daniel went down to fetch it for him (there is broth always ready in this household, the boiling of bones with onions and greens being a very frequent sight in the kitchen), thus leaving me alone with Pearce.

I sat down beside him, just within reach of his breath, which smelled of sulphur. He began to talk, quite lucidly, just as he once did at Bidnold, about the theory of spontaneous generation, in which he has never truly believed but which seems proven by the appearance of the living maggot upon dead matter. 'Is it possible, Merivel,' he asked, 'that the maggot is not spontaneously generated but – as has been hypothesised – emerges from an egg so small it cannot be seen by the human eye?'

'I think it is possible, John.'

'And thus, it would follow, if the human eye cannot see these infinitely small things, there may be other pieces of matter of whose existence we have not yet the slightest perception, would it not?'

'It would.'

He sighed. He was silent for a long while. Then he said:

'It troubles me to take with me to my grave so much that I do not know.'

'I would rather you did not talk about the grave, John,' I said.

'Of course you would,' he said acidly. 'There are many matters, ever since I met you, on which you would have preferred me to remain silent. But that has not been my way. And now, there is one uncertainty I do not wish to carry with me. And that is what is going to happen to my things.'

'What things?'

'Those few that are precious to me. You once called them my "burning coals" in order to mock me.'

Daniel arrived at this moment, thus sparing me the humiliation of having to compose yet another apology to Pearce, the syllables of which I find so difficult to pronounce, when what I longed for was for Pearce to beg my forgiveness for the thoughtless act he was about to commit: the act of leaving me.

Daniel set down a tray, on which had been placed a bowl of broth and a spoon and by the side of this a greenish fruit that Pearce immediately recognised as one of his own pears. He picked it up and felt it in his hand, then held it to his sore nose and sniffed it. 'The perfume of pears,' he said in the rapturous voice that always brought back to my mind our river excursions and Pearce's excess of joy at the sight of a mayfly, 'I have loved for years.'

Daniel grinned at me, then sat down beside him to help him sip the broth. Somewhat to my surprise, Pearce asked him gently to leave so that he could talk to me alone. The boy got up at once, passing me the spoon, and went out.

The broth was hot. I did not want Pearce to burn his mouth on it, so I took up a spoonful and blew upon it before guiding it to his lips. Silence descended upon us for a few moments as we both concentrated on the task of the spoon-feeding. But the effort of taking in sustenance seemed to weary Pearce very quickly and he told me to take the tray away and fetch pen and ink and paper instead.

What I wrote – although I do not have the paper before me, having been instructed to give it to Ambrose – I can remember very exactly, for it was perhaps one of the shortest wills ever made, Pearce's burning coals having diminished, as it were, to a mere few cinders. He bequeathed all his books, including his Bible, to Whittlesea House. His clothes – those threadbare garments that he wore without the least tremor of embarrassment or shame – he offered 'to the inmates of our Hospital, so that they may put on the garments of a true Quaker and be tender towards each other', and the ladle he left to me, 'this fragile thing perchance being of comfort to him sometimes'. And this was all. The last line I was ordered to write stated that 'John Joseph Pearce, Quaker, possesses of his own no other thing or things upon earth.'

When I had written down everything (in the careful script I am capable of if I take extreme care with the position of the quill in my hand) I gave the paper to Pearce and helped him to sign his name. I made no comment upon his gift to me of the ladle, being so saddened and troubled by it that for a short while I could not speak. When I found my voice again, it was to offer Pearce a taste of the green pear, which he declined fearing, he said, that it would give him a pain in his teeth.

SINCE THE NIGHT when Pearce had called out to me on my return from Margaret Fell, I had not visited Katharine. I had made a bargain with God: I would not touch her nor let her come near me again if He would give me Pearce's life.

I knew it to be a futile thing. I knew that Pearce was dying. Yet I kept to it. And Katharine, finding herself abandoned by me, came up to the house from the Airing Court and beat on the door with her hands and screamed out for all the world to hear that I was her lover. And that night, the ninth night of Pearce's illness, I and the Keepers sat quietly at supper, they looking at me sadly but saying nothing until the end of the meal when Ambrose spoke. 'When the time is right for Robert to speak to us,' he said, 'then he will speak to us.' And I nodded. And we all rose and began to clear away the plates and dishes.

They knew that I could not leave Whittlesea until Pearce was gone.

HE DIED IN the quiet time between the Night Keeping and the dawn of the eleventh day.

I was with him, alone.

I closed his mouth. I took up his thin, white hands and

folded them across his chest. And into his hands I put the ladle.

'Look,' I whispered to him, 'the ladle will not be taken from you.'

Then I closed his eyes. And I sat down. And it was then that I was aware of the silence, and I knew it would be there for ever, and that whenever I thought of my friend or spoke to him in my mind, I would hear it again, and where before there had been answering words or messages of guidance or sniffs of disapproval, there would henceforward be only this: the Silence of Pearce.

I sat on the hard chair, leaning forward with my elbows on my knees, and cried. I did not try to stem my tears nor mop them up with any handkerchief or striped dinner napkin, but let them fall onto the floor and onto my thighs and run down my legs.

When I looked up again, there was a milky light at the window and Ambrose and Edmund and Hannah and Eleanor and Daniel were there with me in the room, standing by the bed with their palms pressed together in prayer.

A COFFIN WAS made for Pearce that day by two men from George Fox. It was too large for him, but we put him in it and packed his body round with branches of pear.

We held a wake in the parlour and this wake took the form of an all-night Meeting, during which, as and when we were moved to do so, we spoke of him or said prayers for his soul.

I tried, without saying any words, to gather into me

what I could remember of his wisdom and what came to my mind was his despair at the greed and selfishness of our age which he believed was like a disease or plague, to which hardly any were immune, not even the poets or the playwrights, 'because, Robert, even the creative spirit is whoring, and Piety, the mother, has given birth to Luxury, the wanton Daughter . . .' And these thoughts comforted me a little because through them it came to me that the things which Pearce had loved about the world had been so few – the tenderness of Quakers, the wisdom of William Harvey, the memory of his mother, the growing of trees *en espalier*, the light on a trout stream – that, though he declared himself to be afraid of death, he must also very often have longed for it.

I was trying very hard to imagine him in Paradise (I have frequently tried to envisage my parents here, but all my mind is able to conjure up is the Vauxhall Woods and I am inclined to doubt whether, if Paradise exists, it would resemble a place where Londoners go to have picnics), when Daniel suddenly said: 'It has come to me from the Lord that John Pearce taught me many things by the example of his life and the greatest thing that he taught me was never to be blinded by affection, because it was his way to judge most harshly those he loved most, and so his loving of them never hurt them but only helped to strengthen them.' I looked up and saw that Daniel was looking at me, and Ambrose, too, glanced at me, as if the two of them were waiting for me to speak.

I felt very hot, just as I had at the Meeting where I had

suggested the story-telling and the dancing, and so I suspected that some words were going to come out of me, but did not know that when I spoke them they would reveal to me something that I had not, until I uttered it, understood. I wanted to stand up, but my legs felt very weak, so I continued sitting down and then I said: 'In the silence which has fallen since John died this morning, I have listened and waited. It is as if I have been waiting for some word, not from John, nor from God, but from myself to myself and now it has come . . .'

Still, I did not know precisely what the supposed 'word' was or what I was going to say next. I paused and took out a handkerchief and mopped my brow, and then I said: 'In this quiet, I have understood one thing. And it is this: that all my love for women which, before I came here, was a very trumpeted and tempestuous thing, and even all the love I thought I had for my wife, Celia . . . all these loves were mere deceptions and not love at all, but only vanity and lust, for which I am ashamed. And in all my life I have truly loved only two people on earth, and these two are John Pearce and the King.'

At the shock of hearing the King's name put beside Pearce's, all the Friends raised their eyes and cast upon me their sternest looks. I opened my hands in a gesture of helplessness. 'You will straightway say,' I continued, 'that my love for John Pearce is worthy and my love for the King unworthy and that I should, as indeed John often told me, cast it out from me. But it seems that I cannot. For whatever I do and however far I travel from my former life, I

**And in all my life
I have truly loved
only two people
on earth, and these
two are John Pearce
and the King.**

still find it there. But it is no longer a greedy love. It asks nothing. It is like the love for a dead man; it is like my love for John. For I will see neither man ever again. I will never be with them. All I understand tonight is that these two people I have truly loved – wisely in one particular, unwisely in the other – and that no one else on earth has ever counted as these two have counted with me. And for this knowledge, which may have come to me from the Lord or from some other place, I feel grateful.'

The flush that had come into my face and body subsided after some minutes, despite my awareness that the eyes of all the Friends were still upon me. The air was very close with their displeasure and I expected them to start speaking out against me. But they did not. And I imagined each one of them wrestling with his or her anger and conquering it for the sake of quietness and for the sake of John.

And so the night went on and became morning and at six o'clock, we drank some chocolate and ate some biscuits which seemed to me to taste most strangely of charcoal.

TOWARDS MIDDAY OF the tenth of September, Pearce was put into his grave and the yellow clay of Whittlesea packed tightly around and above him. I had made certain that the ladle was put into the coffin with him before the lid was nailed down. But at the graveside I found myself remembering how, at Cambridge, some cunning thieves calling themselves 'Anglers' had tried to steal it and all Pearce's possessions from him. They worked with a long pole, on the end of which was a hook made of wire, and such a pole had been thrust through Pearce's open window one night while he slept. He had woken up to see a chair moving in a glimmer of moonlight three feet off the floor and floating out through the window. 'It was only,' he told me, 'when the pole came back into the room and I saw it move towards my ladle that I understood there were villains at work and not ghosts. And so I cried out angrily, and my shouting frightened them and they ran away.' He laughed when he had told me this story and then he said: 'Perhaps it is always easier to frighten away the living than it is to frighten away the dead? What do you think, Merivel?'

But, I cannot remember what I answered.

The Gustav Sonata

The cold spring of the year

ANTON ARRIVED AT the kindergarten in the cold spring
of the year.

He came into the schoolroom and stood by the door,
crying. None of the children had seen this boy before.
One of the teachers, Fräulein Frick, went to him and
took his hand and knelt down and began talking to
him, but he didn't seem to hear her. He just kept on
weeping.

Fräulein Frick beckoned to Gustav. Gustav didn't particularly want to be the boy chosen to comfort this
weeping child, but Fräulein Frick urged him to come
towards her and said to Anton, 'This is Gustav. Gustav is
going to be your friend. He will take you to the sandbox
and you can build a castle together before we begin our
lessons.'

Anton looked down at Gustav, who was slightly smaller
than he was.

**This is Gustav.
Gustav is going
to be your friend.**

Gustav said to him, 'My mother says it's better not to cry. She says you have to *master yourself*.'

Anton appeared so startled by this that his sobbing stopped abruptly.

'There,' said Fräulein Frick. 'That's good. Go with Gustav, then.' She produced a handkerchief and wiped Anton's cheeks. The boy's face was a hectic pink, his eyes big pools of darkness. His body was trembling.

Gustav led him over to the sandbox. Anton's small hand felt burning hot. Gustav said, 'What kind of castle do you want to build?' But the boy couldn't answer. So Gustav gave him a spade and said, 'I like castles with moats. Shall we start on the moat?'

Gustav marked out a circle and they began digging. A few other children clustered round them, staring at the new boy.

BEFORE ANTON ARRIVED, Gustav had had no close friends at the kindergarten. There was a girl who amused him called Isabel. She liked to climb onto the work tables and jump off again, landing like a gymnast with her feet together and her arms outspread. She always brought her pet mouse to school in a wooden cage and Gustav was one of the few children allowed to stroke the mouse. But Isabel was too exhausting to play with for long. She had to be the Queen of every game.

All his life, Gustav would remember vividly that first morning spent with Anton. They didn't talk very much. It was as if Anton was so exhausted by his weeping that he *couldn't* talk. He just followed Gustav around and sat very close to him at the work table and watched what he did and tried to copy him. When Gustav asked him where he'd come from, he said, 'From Bern. We had a house in Bern, but now we've only got an apartment in Matzlingen.'

Gustav said, 'The place where I live is very small. We don't even have a kitchen table. Have you got a kitchen table?'

'Yes,' said Anton, 'we've got a kitchen table. I was sick all over it at breakfast because I didn't want to come here.'

Later, Anton asked Gustav, 'Have you got a piano?'

'No,' said Gustav.

'We've got a piano and I can play it. I can play "Für Elise". Not the fast bit, but the first section.'

'What's "Für Elise"?' asked Gustav.

'Beethoven,' said Anton.

Perhaps it was the idea of Anton playing the piano with his small hands, or perhaps it was when Anton told him that his surname was Zwiebel, which was identical to the word for 'onion', and made you feel sorry for him; whatever it was, there was something about Anton which made Gustav feel that he had to protect him.

The following day, Anton was crying again when he arrived. Gustav saw Fräulein Frick coming towards him, but he stood in her way and said that Anton would be all right with him. He led him to the Nature Table and showed him the silkworms that were being reared in a grocery box with a perforated lid. He said, 'In the box we had before, the holes were too big and the silkworms climbed out of them.'

'Where did they go?' asked Anton through his tears.

'They went all over the place,' said Gustav. 'We tried to find them and put them back, but some of them got trodden on. Treading on a silkworm is disgusting.'

Gustav saw Anton smile, but then his tears welled up again and he put his face in his hands.

Gustav said, 'What are you crying for?'

Anton stammered that he was crying for the loss of his friends at his old kindergarten in Bern.

'Are they dead?' asked Gustav.

'No. But I'll never see them again. I'm in this place now.'

Gustav said, 'I think it's stupid to cry for them, then. Isn't your mother angry that you keep crying?'

Anton took his hands away from his face and stared at Gustav. 'No,' he said, 'she understands that I'm unhappy.'

'Well,' said Gustav, 'I think it's a bit stupid. You're here now, so you just have to get on with it.'

The bell rang for the beginning of morning lessons. Anton followed Gustav to one of the work tables. Pieces of grey sugar paper were put in front of them and boxes of crayons and they were told to start the day by drawing a picture of anything they liked.

Anton's tears slowly speckled the paper, like fat raindrops, but after five or six minutes, he stopped crying.

'What are you going to draw?' he asked Gustav.

'I'm going to draw my mother,' he said.

'Is your mother beautiful?'

'I don't know. She's just my mother. She works at the cheese co-operative, making Emmental.'

Fräulein Frick rapped on her desk with a ruler. 'You know the rules,' she said. 'When we're drawing pictures, we're silent. We talk silently to our pictures, not to each other.'

Gustav wanted Emilie to be sitting at the kitchen shelf in his picture, so he drew the shelf first, a kind of oblong, resting on air. He coloured it brown. Then he began on Emilie's face, not a round thing, but a narrow kind of shape he didn't know how to make. He saw straight away that what he'd drawn was *too* narrow. He put his hand up and Fräulein Frick came over and Gustav said, 'This was meant to be a face, but it looks like an ice-cream cone.'

'Never mind,' said Fräulein Frick. 'Why don't you make it a cone? Put some nice strawberry ice cream into it.'

There was something amusing about this – that Emilie Perle could suddenly become a cornet. Gustav whispered to Anton, 'I was going to draw my Mutti but she went wrong. Now she's an ice cream.'

And this was the first time that he heard Anton laugh. And it was the kind of laugh that couldn't be resisted; you had to join in, and suddenly the two boys couldn't stop giggling. Gustav suspected that Fräulein Frick was watching them sternly, but she said nothing and when he looked up at her – mastering his giggling at last – her expression wasn't stern at all, but just rather sweetly amused.

Gustav selected a pink crayon and drew a scribble of

ice cream on his cornet. Then he looked over to see what Anton was drawing. He was using only a black crayon. He'd laid a small ruler on the sugar paper and drawn a line all the way round it. Inside the perfectly ruled shape was a series of black lines of differing lengths. Gustav knew what the thing was meant to be: it was a piano.

GUSTAV TOLD EMILIE about Anton's laugh. He said, 'I like hearing it.'

In the night, he began trying to think up funny stories to tell Anton, so that he'd be able to hear his laughter all through the day. And then he had an idea which surprised him – he decided to show Anton the treasure in the cigar box. He would show him because he thought that Anton would see that it was a collection worth hoarding. But Gustav wouldn't risk taking it in to the kindergarten. He said to Emilie, 'Could we invite Anton Zwiebel for tea?'

'Zwiebel?' said Emilie. 'That's a very peculiar name.'

'He can't help his name,' said Gustav.

'No. But names are important. When I first met your father and he told me his surname was Perle, I thought how beautiful it was and how I would like to become Frau Perle.'

Gustav looked up at his mother. She was undoing her scraggly hair from the red handkerchief she tied it in for work, letting her hair fall round her face. Then, she smoothed it and patted it, as if, right then and there, she was preparing once again for that first meeting with a man called Erich Perle.

'On a Wednesday, we could invite him?' said Gustav. 'On your half-day off.'

'Anton Zwiebel. Well, I've never heard a name like that before. But yes, we can invite him – if his parents agree. I could make a Nusstorte, assuming I can get the walnuts at this time of year . . .'

'He might not like walnuts.'

'Too bad. If he doesn't like them, he doesn't have to eat the Nusstorte.'

IT WAS LATE spring by the time the invitation to tea went out. It was agreed that Anton would walk from school to Unter der Egg with Gustav and that his father would collect him from Emilie's apartment at six o'clock. The father, it appeared, was a banker, who'd worked for a large national bank in Bern and now worked for a smaller branch of that bank in Matzlingen. The reasons for the move weren't explained. All Anton said was that everybody in the family missed living in Bern. Herr Zwiebel, the banker, missed his big bank; Frau Zwiebel, who was a housewife, missed the wonderful shops and Anton missed his old friends.

Every May, in the courtyard at the back of the apartment, a white cherry tree bloomed. In this spring of 1948, perhaps because of the steady rains that had fallen at the end of winter, the flowers on the cherry were so abundant that the branches of the tree hung low towards the stones of the yard.

Gustav's window, where he played with his tin train, overlooked the cherry tree, and he saw how the residents who went in and out of the building by that route, almost invariably paused and stood staring at the tree, with its cargo of beauty, and sometimes reached out to it, as they might have reached out, in yearning, to a lost person. Emilie said that there had once been cherry trees at the front of the building, all along Unter der Egg, but they'd been torn out and now there was just this one tree in the courtyard. She said, 'The tree is special for people, because it's lasted through all the upheaval – as certain things sometimes seem to do.'

'What things?' asked Gustav.

'Well,' said Emilie, 'like that white dog you pointed out in the rubble of Berlin. It had survived.'

'You said it might have found a good master or it might have starved to death.'

'I know I did. But the point was, when everything around it had been destroyed, it was still there for a while. It had hung on.'

So the Wednesday afternoon of the tea arrived. Gustav enjoyed walking home in the sunshine with Anton. He felt proud, in a way that he couldn't explain.

When Anton was introduced to Emilie, Gustav saw that his mother stared at him for longer than she would normally stare at people she met for the first time, and Gustav wondered what was going through her mind. She said, 'You and Gustav go and play in his room for a little while, then we'll have tea and Nusstorte. I hope you like Nusstorte.'

'I don't know what it is,' said Anton.

'Ah,' said Emilie. 'Well, Gustav will explain to you.'

They went to Gustav's room, where, at this time of the day, the sun was falling in a diagonal across the window, and Gustav said, 'Nusstorte is a sort of pastry thing, with caramel and walnuts inside.'

But Anton wasn't listening. They were standing at the windowsill, next to the metal train and Anton was staring down at the white cherry tree. He said, 'Can we go down there?'

'To play in the courtyard?'

'I want to see that tree.'

'It's just a cherry tree,' said Gustav.

'Can't we go down there?'

'We'll have to ask Mutti.'

Emilie said, 'All right, but I'll come with you. I don't want you making a noise on the stairs. You remember Herr Nieder is very ill, Gustav?'

'Herr Nieder is our neighbour,' said Gustav to Anton. 'He's dying.'

'Oh,' said Anton. 'Has he got a piano?'

'I don't know. Has he, Mutti?'

'A piano?' said Emilie. 'Why do you ask?'

'Well,' said Anton, 'if he does, I could play "Für Elise" for him.'

'He might not want you to play "Für Elise",' said Gustav.

'He would. Everybody likes me to play that.'

'Well, not now,' said Emilie. 'Let's go down very quietly, shall we?'

So they arrived in the courtyard and Anton stared at the cherry tree and his dark eyes widened. He ran to the tree and began to hop from one foot to the other and then to jump up and down, uttering little cries of joy.

Gustav stood very still, watching Anton. He decided that there was something connecting Anton's joy at the sight of the cherry blossom to his early morning weeping at the kindergarten, but he couldn't say what. He went towards his friend and took his hand and together they began to skip round and round the tree, laughing until they were out of breath. Gustav had no idea exactly *why* he was skipping, but he knew that Anton knew and that seemed to be enough.

One or two of the apartment residents arrived in the courtyard and stopped to smile at the two boys dancing round the old cherry. Later, when Anton had gone home, Emilie said, 'I suppose there may not be any cherry trees in Bern. It's unlikely, but one can't say for sure. Perhaps he had never seen one before?'

'I don't know,' said Gustav.

'I think he is a nice boy,' said Emilie, 'but of course he is a Jew.'

'What's a Jew?' asked Gustav.

'Ah,' said Emilie. 'The Jews are the people your father died trying to save.'

'Swear in blood'

THIS WAS THE new, wonderful thing: skating.

Frau Zwiebel, whose first name was Adriana, had once

been a 'hopeful' in the skating world. At fifteen she'd won a competition in Bern. She told Gustav that this had been one of the happiest moments of her life. She'd expected to go on and win more prizes, but at sixteen she moved into 'a different category' and the girls she was competing against were what she called 'full-blown professionals, with dragons for mothers and steel for sinews'. And so no more prizes came her way, but she still loved skating, for its own sake, and when she heard about the new rink opening in Matzlingen – a covered rink with smooth, manufactured ice and a huge gramophone which played Swiss folk music and American jazz, and a café counter which sold drinks and pretzels – she said to Anton, 'Let's go on Sunday afternoons. We can take Gustav. I'll pay for us all.'

She had a beautiful glide. And she could still gather momentum for a perfect lutz and land with grace. Adriana Zwiebel dressed herself in woollen leggings, a short tartan skirt and a green leather jacket. The eyes of the men at the rink followed her as she made her elegant turns, with her arms held out like a dancer's and her dark hair tied in a ponytail flicking and flouncing as she moved.

Seven-year-old Anton and seven-year-old Gustav watched her, too, not so much because she was beautiful, but because they knew they could learn from her. Anton was naturally good at skating and Gustav was not, but Gustav set himself to master everything Anton could do and, in time, everything that Adriana could do – however distant this goal might be. He fell over frequently, but he never cried, though the ice was hard, the hardest surface his bones had ever met. He taught himself to laugh instead. Laughing was a bit like crying. It was a strange convulsion; it just came from a different bit of your mind. The trick was to move the crying out of that bit and let the laughter in. And so he'd pick himself up and carry on, laughing.

At the end of the afternoon, he and Anton would do one circuit of what they called their 'mad dash'. They would hold hands and skate in synchronisation as fast as they could round the rink's outer edge. They came to be known by the rink regulars as 'the laughing boys'. At this time, Gustav was one inch shorter than Anton.

IT WAS AT the skating rink, where Anton and Gustav were allowed to buy hot chocolate, that Gustav learned about something 'nobody ever mentions'.

Anton told him that he had once had a baby sister, named Romola. He said, 'I can't remember her very well. She just stayed being a baby and then she died.'

'Why did she?' asked Gustav.

'That's what nobody talks about.'

'Was she killed by some robbers?'

'I can't remember any robbers.'

'They could have come with a hatchet, or something?'

'I don't think they did. I was three. I would have remembered robbers, wouldn't I? I think my sister just died in her cot and then she was buried, and some time after that my father got ill and was put into a hospital. My mother told me he was ill because Romola had died and he had to be left in peace, to recover.'

Gustav and Anton looked out at Adriana, still on the ice, still turning and leaping, as if she would never weary of her own wonderful grace.

'What about her?' asked Gustav. 'Wasn't your mother ill, too, after the death of baby Romola?'

'No,' said Anton. 'My mother is never ill. She's never even tired. Except when we had to leave Bern. She said she was tired then. I expect it was the thought of moving all the furniture. We couldn't leave it behind, because my parents are very fond of furniture.'

'So why did you leave Bern?'

'Something to do with my father's job. I think the bank in Bern thought – after he'd been ill for a long time because of my sister dying – that he'd be happier in a smaller bank, and so we came to Matzlingen.'

'And you cried at the kindergarten.'

'And you drew your Mutti as an ice cream!'

They laughed then, but Anton stopped laughing suddenly and said, 'You must never, ever tell anybody about Romola, Gustav. Swear in blood.'

'What d'you mean, swear in blood?'

'You have to. We have to cut our arms with our skate blades and mix the blood together and then you have to swear.'

'All right.'

All his life, Gustav would recall that it's difficult to make a cut in your arm with an ice skate. The blades look sharp, but they're not sharp enough for easy cutting. 'We made a hash of it,' he would tell people. 'We couldn't get the blood to come. But then it did because we made the cuts too deep and we were both in pain, but we had to cover this up.'

Strangely beautiful

LATER IN THEIR lives, they asked themselves, was it 'within reason', the game they chose to play in Davos? They knew it was strange. But in the strangeness of it lay its fascination and its beauty.

It was on the second day that they found the stone path leading up through the pine trees into darker forest. The path was wide but overgrown. Wild strawberries were growing at its edge: tiny points of red, like beads of blood among the bandages of green leaves. Gustav and Anton stopped to gather a few of these and eat them. The texture was rough, but the taste was sweet.

They knew the path was leading somewhere. There were narrow ruts in the stone surface, as if, long ago, carts and carriages had passed this way. Overhead, the firs crowded out the light and they felt the air become colder. A wind got up and began sighing in the trees.

'Are you frightened?' asked Anton. 'Shall we go back?'

'No,' said Gustav.

They were high up now. At moments, there were glimpses of Davos village, far below. Then the path opened out and became a plateau and on the plateau was an enormous building.

It was ruined. Part of its roof was missing and the glass in most of the windows was broken. Along its southerly edge ran a wooden veranda, cracked and faded by the sunlight. At its back, pressed against the forest, was a brick outhouse with a vast chimney stack rearing up into the sky.

Gustav and Anton stood still and stared. A rusted chain, attached to wooden posts, had been strung across the path – a token attempt, it seemed, to keep people away from a place which had so obviously fallen into dereliction. Gustav listened for the bark of a guard dog, but everything was silent, except for the movement of the trees, like the sound of laboured breathing.

The boys climbed over the chain. All that remained of the entrance to the building was a stone portico with the words *Sankt Alban* engraved above the place where the door had been. They passed underneath this into a small, dark space and then through this space into an enormous room, filled with light. In ranks, along the back wall, facing towards the light, were twenty or thirty iron beds.

'Hospital,' said Anton.

'Sanatorium,' corrected Gustav. 'Where people came to recover from tuberculosis. Or to die.'

'Maybe they all died,' said Anton. 'That's why it was abandoned.'

They walked slowly along the light-filled room. They began to notice other things: rusty oxygen cylinders clamped to the walls, coils of rubber tubing, oxygen masks, buckets, kidney bowls, stained mattresses, a nurse's trolley still set out with brown glass bottles, a stethoscope lying in the rubble.

Anton picked up the stethoscope, dusted it against his Aertex shirt, and hung it round his neck.

'Doctor,' he said. 'You're my nurse, Gustav. Fetch the trolley.'

'We haven't got any patients,' said Gustav.

'Yes, we have. Can't you see them?'

'No.'

'On the beds. We're going to bring them alive again.'

So THAT WAS how it began, the game of choosing who, among the sufferers of Sankt Alban, lived or died. They gave the patients names: Hans, Margaret, Frau Merligen, Frau Bünden, Herr Mollis, Herr Weiss . . .

Hans and Margaret were children. Doctor Zwiebel and Nurse Perle were going to have to work especially hard to bring them back to the world. They found the best mattresses for them, those least eaten away by mould. They searched the rest of the building for things that might comfort them: pillows and torn blankets, chamber pots and hot-water bottles.

'And,' said Anton, 'we can bring them toys from the box in the chalet.'

'Yes,' said Gustav, 'except . . .'

'Except what?'

'Won't your parents think this is odd? They might not want us to play here.'

'We won't tell them,' said Anton.

'Where will they think we are?'

'Just "exploring". On holidays, when she doesn't want me around, my mother's always saying "Why don't you go *exploring*, Anton?" We'll tell them we're building a camp in the forest. And anyway, they'll be fucking.'

'What's fucking?'

'It's what they like to do on holiday. They go to bed and take their clothes off and kiss and scream things out. It's called fucking.'

Gustav thought about this. He said, 'I don't think my mother's ever done that. She just goes to bed and reads magazines.'

THEY FORGOT ABOUT time. To get back to the chalet for lunch, when they heard a midday bell chiming in the village, they had to go racing through the sunlit rooms, down the steps and back onto the steep path. Not stopping, now, to collect strawberries, they ran fast under the canopy of sighing trees, down and down towards the slender pines, until they emerged behind the house and saw Monsieur in the meadow, scattering grain for the hens.

They found Armin and Adriana, sipping wine on the terrace, beside the trough of geraniums. On the table was a dish of meats and pickles and cheese.

'You're out of breath,' said Adriana, as Anton and Gustav sat down. 'Where have you been?'

'Exploring,' they both said together.

'Exploring where?' said Armin.

'In the forest,' said Anton. 'We're making a camp.'

'A camp?' said Adriana, frowning. 'What kind of *camp*?'

'Just a den. It's not finished yet.'

'Can your father and I come and see it?'

'No.'

'Why not?'

'It's not finished. And anyway, it's ours.'

'Good for you,' said Armin with a smile. 'Now have some meat.'

'THAT TIME. THAT Sankt Alban time . . .' they would say, later in their lives. 'That was a thing we've never forgotten.' And sometimes, they would add, 'We've never forgotten it, because we thought we really had power over life and death.'

On the first day, they made sure that Frau Merligen, Frau Bünden, Herr Mollis and Herr Weiss were comfortable, while they took the pulses of Hans and Margaret and gave oxygen to Hans, who was dying faster than the others. They found some old bamboo and wickerwork recliners and pushed the sick children out onto the veranda, where the sun was strong and where there was shelter from the wind. From the chalet box, they'd brought a rag doll for Margaret and a tambourine for Hans. They told Hans to rattle the tambourine if he felt that death was coming near.

'What shall we do if Hans dies?' asked Gustav.

Anton thought for a moment, then said, 'That outhouse

with the chimney – it's probably where they burned dead people. We'll put him in there.'

'I don't want him to die,' said Gustav.

'No. I don't either. I tell you what. Shall I be him? You can have the stethoscope and I'll lie on the recliner. If I feel I'm dying, I'll bang the tambourine and you have to come and give me resuscitation.'

'All right. I'll stay with Frau Bünden for a while. She's not looking good. Then you bang the tambourine and I'll come.'

Gustav decided that Frau Bünden resembled Frau Teller, who kept the flower stall on Unter der Egg. She was too young to die. He sat on her bed and told her to think about all the flowers she was going to return to: roses and lilies, tulips, daffodils, edelweiss and blue gentians. He said, 'You're safe in Davos now, Frau Bünden. It's the best place in Switzerland for you. What you have to do is *concentrate* on getting well. Don't think about the TB, right? Think about flowers.'

Frau Bünden said, 'I'm very weak, Nurse Perle. My lungs are full of blood.'

'I know they are. I'm not Nurse Perle now, by the way, I'm Doctor Perle. Doctor Zwiebel and I are going to save you. You just have to believe us. All right? This is Davos.'

Then he heard the rattle of the tambourine and said, 'Forgive me a moment, Frau Bünden, I have to go and look after Hans. I've got to make sure Hans doesn't die.'

Gustav adjusted the stethoscope round his neck and went out onto the veranda. Hans was lying very still, with his eyes closed. The sun shone on his dark hair and on his soft limbs, curled on the recliner. Doctor Perle knelt down beside him and stroked his arm. 'Hans,' he said, 'are you dying?'

'Can't you see I'm dying?' said Hans. 'Put your lips on my lips and revive me, Nurse Perle . . .'

'I'm not Nurse Perle, I'm Doctor Perle now,' said Gustav, 'and I'm not putting my lips on your lips.'

'You have to,' said Hans, 'or I'm gone. You'll have to burn my body in the outhouse . . .'

'I'm not doing that lip thing.'

'Gustav,' said Anton, sitting up suddenly, 'don't be a baby. This is how you revive someone. You put your mouth on their mouth. We learned it in school. Don't you remember? So, go on.'

Hans lay down again. He began to moan.

'Hush,' said Doctor Perle. 'I'm going to revive you now. Here.'

Anton turned his face towards Gustav. Slowly and reluctantly, Gustav brought his mouth to Anton's and lightly touched his lips. He felt Anton lift his arm and put it round his neck and bring his head nearer, so that the two mouths were now pressed hard against each other and Gustav could feel Anton's face, burning hot against his own. He'd thought he would pull away at once, but he stayed there. He liked the feel of Anton gathering his head in his arm. He closed his eyes. He felt that no moment of his life had been as strangely beautiful as this one.

Then he pulled away. 'Are you all right, Hans?' he whispered. 'Are you going to live?'

He liked the feel of Anton gathering his head in his arm. He closed his eyes. He felt that no moment of his life had been as strangely beautiful as this one.

'Yes,' murmured Hans. 'Thanks to you. I'm going to live, thanks to you.'

SANKT ALBAN TOOK over their minds.

The time they spent with Adriana and Armin – going for walks, swimming at the pool, taking the cable car higher up the mountain towards the Schatzalp, shopping for souvenirs, collecting eggs for Monsieur, lying in the sun, eating meals on the chalet terrace – all these things, enjoyable as they were, became infected with ordinariness. At every moment, they longed to be back at the sanatorium, back in the beautiful pretend world of the dying.

One day, they decided that Frau Bünden had died. They carried her, wrapped in a torn rug, on a wicker recliner, to the outhouse. Its door was hanging on one hinge and they pushed this and went in. They put Frau Bünden down. The space in which they found themselves was black with coal dust. At the far end of it was a metal door, and when they opened this, they saw that it was the door to an enormous oven, still choked with ash.

'I told you,' said Anton. 'This is where they burned the dead. I suppose they had to burn everything, to stop the infection spreading.'

'Are we going to put Frau Bünden in there?'

'Yes,' said Anton. 'And burn her.'

'We haven't got any matches.'

'We can bring some from the chalet.'

* * *

THEY CAME BACK the following day with matches and newspaper. They fetched logs from an old, rotting wood-pile. Before they put Frau Bünden into the oven, Anton said, 'Wait, Gustav. You know there's going to be smoke from the chimney if we make a fire? Then, Monsieur or somebody might come and send us away.'

'We can't leave her to rot,' said Gustav.

They stared at the recliner not knowing what they should do. After a few moments, Anton said, 'Listen! Hans is rattling his tambourine. He needs us. We'll burn Frau Bünden some other time.'

'I know what,' suggested Gustav. 'Let's burn all the dead ones on our last day. We can light the fire and then just run back to the chalet.'

'How many dead ones are there going to be?' asked Anton.

'We haven't decided,' said Gustav.

They went out onto the veranda, glad to breathe in the scent of the firs and feel the sunlight on their faces. They stood looking down at the village far below and Gustav thought with dismay of the scant time remaining in Davos, and of his miserable return to the apartment on Unter der Egg. On an impulse – not knowing that he was going to do this – he turned to Anton and said, 'I don't want to go home. Something bad happens there.'

'What happens?'

'It's a secret, right? I've never told anyone and you must never tell a single other soul.'

'I won't. Don't look so panicked, Gustav.'

'All right. *Swear* you won't tell?'

'I swear.'

'OK, it's this, then. There's a man in our block, Ludwig, who tries to make me touch him.'

'Tries to make you touch him?'

'Yes. Touch his penis. I hate him. It makes me feel disgusting.'

Anton looked hard at Gustav. 'Did you do it?' he asked. 'Did you touch his dick?'

'No. I never would. I wish he was dead.'

'All right,' said Anton. 'Let's kill him. What's his name? Ludwig? We'll give him TB and let him die and then burn him.'

'Promise you won't tell, Anton?'

'Of course I won't. I've sworn, haven't I? But Ludwig's got to die.'

They selected another recliner. They put a badly stained mattress onto it and threw down a torn piece of grey fabric, which might once have been part of a curtain.

'There you are,' said Anton. 'Ludwig.'

Anton put the stethoscope in his ears and bent down towards Ludwig, to listen to the murmur of his lungs. 'Ah,' he said, after a while, 'I'm sorry to tell you, Ludwig, there is no improvement. Doctor Perle, is there any of Ludwig's special medicine left?'

'No,' said Doctor Perle. 'None. I can order more from Geneva, but I'm afraid it will arrive too late.'

'Did you hear that, Ludwig?' said Doctor Zwiebel. 'What we suggest is that you prepare yourself for death.'

At this moment, the sun went in. The rag covering Ludwig became a dark shadow, seemingly without form.

Gustav shivered. 'If we're going to kill Ludwig,' he said, 'I think Hans should be saved.'

ON THEIR LAST day, they lit the fire in the oven. They tried to put Frau Bünden into the oven, lying dead on her bamboo recliner, but the recliner wouldn't fit through the oven door, so they took her off the bed, wrapped in her rug, and threw her in. The wool rug seemed greedy for the flame and hissed and crackled like a firework.

Then Anton took an axe they'd found near the woodpile and began to break up the recliner.

'Why are you doing that?' asked Gustav.

'You'll see. It's clever. The bamboo stalks will look like human bones, then we'll have proper bodies to burn.'

It was hard work. They took it in turns to heft the axe. Then they arranged the bamboo pieces, still joined here and there to the wickerwork threads, into skeletal patterns. They looked strangely real, with their sad sinews of wicker hanging off them, representing all that remained of their emaciated flesh.

'They're good,' said Gustav. 'Very good, Anton. Except they've got no heads.'

It was at this moment that they heard, still some distance away, the sound of a fire engine's siren.

'*Scheisse!*' said Anton. 'They'll find us and cart us off to prison. Never mind about the heads. Let's call this one Ludwig and put him in, and then we'll run.'

They took up the bamboo skeleton and hurled it in, piece by piece.

'Die, Ludwig!' cried Anton.

'Die, Ludwig!' repeated Gustav.

The siren sound was very near now. Anton and Gustav ran out of the sanatorium of Sankt Alban and down the forest path, then catapulted themselves into the undergrowth of the woods and hid there, waiting for the fire engine to pass. They clung together, afraid, yet filled with exaltation. They could hear each other's hearts beating.

It was only after a while that Gustav remembered Hans, still lying on the veranda. 'What about Hans?' he whispered.

'We can't go back,' said Anton. 'We have to pretend Hans just walked out of there.'

'Without his tambourine?'

'Yes.'

Gustav was silent for a moment, then he said, 'We didn't say goodbye to him, Anton. And I know I'm going to think about the tambourine. Aren't you? I'm just going to imagine it being there for evermore.'

'He knows how much I love him'

SOME DREAMS ENDURE.

Anton Zwiebel said of his own dream of becoming a concert pianist that the word *endurance* was ironically appropriate to it, because it entailed so much suffering.

After the first piano competition in Bern, at which he'd come last in his group of five finalists, Anton had subjected himself to eight or nine further competitions, where once again he'd done well enough in the heats to reach the final and then faltered when he had to play on a grand stage. He had never once been declared the winner, nor even the runner-up.

Adriana took Anton to the doctor, to try to find a cure for what she said were just 'nerves'. He was prescribed calming drugs of different kinds and differing strengths, but none helped him to conquer his terror on the concert platform. He still played badly when it came to the moment of needing to play well.

He sometimes raged about being 'tested' in this way. It was Gustav who had to listen to his anger. Anton said, 'It has to be you, Gustav. I can't let my parents see me behaving like a wild dog. I've already let them down enough. They paid tons of money for lessons with Herr Edelstein and yet more for competition entry fees, and they expect results. Whereas you –'

'You're right,' said Gustav. 'I don't care if you win or not. All I mind about is that not winning makes you unhappy.'

ONE DAY, WHEN Gustav and Anton were both eighteen and went to the ice rink after school, Anton said that he didn't want to skate, he wanted to talk. So they sat in the rink café, drinking beer, while the skaters kept gliding and turning and jumping and falling at their backs, and Anton said, 'I can't go on with this dream of fame. It's killing me.'

They talked for a long time, getting drunk on beer. Anton said that he'd never abandon music, it was too important a part of his life, but that he had to give up competing. 'I just want to play the piano, because playing the piano is a beautiful thing to do,' he said. 'I played Beethoven's "Moonlight" Sonata over and over the other evening, when my parents were out at some dinner. And I know this is a schmaltzy piece, but each time I played it, it moved me more and more and I played it better and better, until I was crying and playing at the same time. The keyboard was soaked, but I didn't care. I felt I was transfigured, or something. And that's when I thought, *this* is what I want – to be moved by my own playing, but not have to be on a stage and move a thousand other people. I know you'll understand.'

Gustav looked at Anton's face, bright pink from the cold of the ice and from the emotion welling up inside him. He reached out and put the back of his hand against Anton's cheek.

'Of course I understand,' he said. 'I'm glad you've decided this. I was beginning to be afraid for you.'

'Were you? But there's one other thing facing me, Gustav. How am I going to tell my parents? Especially my mother. How am I going to tell her that all her hopes for me are going to be crushed?'

Gustav turned and looked out at the skaters and he thought how the ice rink had always been a place of laughter and joy, and the laughter he could remember best was Adriana's.

'I'll tell her for you,' he said. 'If you want me to. I can explain it.'

'Isn't that asking too much of you?' said Anton.

'No.'

'She might accept it better, coming from you. She knows you always see into the heart of things.'

'Perhaps . . .'

'But she may get upset, Gustav. If she does, just put your arms round her.'

GUSTAV WENT TO Fribourgstrasse on an early summer afternoon, when Armin was at his office. Sunlight filled the room. Adriana was pruning her geraniums. He asked her for a drink of water.

He sat down with Adriana on one of the chintzy sofas and she took his hand in hers. 'You know I'm always delighted to see you, Gustav,' she said, 'but something tells me that you're bringing me bad news. Am I right?'

'Yes,' said Gustav. 'And I hate to be doing this to you and to Armin, but Anton's counting on me.'

Adriana let go of Gustav's hand. 'Has he got a girl pregnant?' she said. 'Is that it?'

'No. Not as far as I know.'

'Well, then, you'd better tell me what it is.'

Adriana let Gustav speak and didn't interrupt. He tried to explain Anton's feelings *as though he were Anton*. And he found that this wasn't difficult, because he knew these feelings so well. As he talked, he felt his face grow pink with emotion. He almost felt that he might cry.

When he'd finished, Adriana lit a cigarette. She smoked and said nothing for a while. Then, she leaned forwards with her elbows on her knees. She said, 'I had another child, Gustav. A little girl we called Romola, who died at the age of one. Anton will barely remember her. But Armin and I . . . of course she's with us in our thoughts all the time. And I suppose that all the hopes we may have had for our two children we've put onto the sole survivor, our beloved Anton. It's in our nature to strive, to want to see our children succeed, and what more wonderful thing could there be in the world than to become a famous pianist? Music is so important in a human life. It finds a space inside us that nothing else touches.'

Gustav was unsure of what he was expected to say. He began thinking about Romola and the day at the rink when he and Anton had cut their arms with skate blades, to mingle their blood and swear their secrecy. He could remember the pain of the cutting and the strange feeling of Anton's blood pooling in a slit in his arm.

After Adriana had smoked some more in silence, she put out her cigarette and said, 'I've imagined it so many times, Gustav – the moment when Anton would conquer his fear and begin to perform on a world stage. He has the talent to do it. We all know that he does. But now you're telling me that day is never going to come?'

'Yes. I'm telling you. That day is never going to come.'

'I can't bear it, Gustav!'

'I know it's hard. But perhaps you knew what Anton was feeling all along and this is really no surprise to you?'

'I *didn't* know! Armin had some anxieties about it. I told him he was being pessimistic: I told him Anton would conquer his fears in time. But I was wrong. And I should have seen it. We paid enough for medication. I'm his mother and I've been obtuse. I've pushed too hard and made Anton suffer. And now all our dreams collapse . . .'

Adriana began to weep. Gustav remembered what Anton had said about putting his arms round her, so he moved closer to her on the sofa and held her and she laid her head on his chest and allowed herself to cry. Gustav stroked her hair and said, 'You mustn't think Anton blames you in any way. He doesn't. He said to me, "We were all in this folly together." That was the word he used – folly. And he included me in that. Because he knows . . . well . . . he knows how much I love him. I love you all, Adriana. I wish I had a family like yours.'

When he found that this was what he'd said – this thing about love – Gustav couldn't suppress tears of his own. He and Adriana clung together, rocking and crying. The moment was so intense, it created in Gustav a feeling of overwhelming sexual yearning. He lifted Adriana's face and held it close to his and she whispered his name, Gustav . . . He kissed her mouth. He expected her to pull away from him, but she didn't. She returned the kiss and Gustav's head swam. He thought that he might lose consciousness. He knew that what he was doing was pure, exquisite sin.

He forced himself out of the moment and back into the sunlit room, where the white net curtains moved lazily at an open window. He drew back from Adriana and laid her head gently against the sofa cushions.

'I'm sorry,' he whispered. 'That was wrong of me. Will you forgive me? Please forgive me and don't hate me, Adriana. And please don't tell Anton.'

Adriana looked at Gustav tenderly. She wiped away her tears. She stroked his burning face. She said, 'That was a beautiful kiss, Gustav. And we all love you very much. I hope you know that. Anton and Armin and I, we love you very much.'

THAT AUTUMN, GUSTAV went away from Matzlingen, for the only significant time in his life, to begin his catering course at Burgdorf.

Anton Zwiebel became a piano teacher.

During Gustav's first vacation from his college, he went to a pupils' concert at the junior school where Anton worked. He saw not only how hard the young children tried with their music, but also how clearly they loved and worshipped Anton. After the pupils had played, they would rush to Anton's side and open their arms to be hugged by him. Gustav saw him as a kind of Pied Piper of Hamelin, with all the enchanted children clustered round him. And he thought, I am one of them; I am enchanted, too. I will follow Anton wherever he leads me – even into a dark cave.

* * *

AT FIFTY NOW, Anton had become head of the Music Department in the much expanded Protestant Academy of Sankt Johann, where once he and Gustav had studied. He was a handsome man with thick, curly hair, greying at the temples, a wounding smile and an infectious laugh which Gustav never tired of hearing.

Gustav knew that women were seduced by Anton and that he enjoyed, to some extent, his power over them. But Anton told Gustav that he never let himself fall in love. He said the idea of living with a woman was 'inimical' to him. He said that making music on the piano would always be the most important thing in his life and the idea that there would be 'this wife-person, this stranger' eavesdropping on his piano practice filled him with horror. Gustav reminded Anton that he always played for him and for his parents, not minding if he made mistakes in front of them, but he replied simply, 'You're not strangers.'

'But your wife would be?'

'Yes. In certain ways, I think she'd remain one.'

Gustav watched with attention Anton's repeated refusal to let any of the women in his life believe she *belonged* to him. They might stay a night or two at his apartment, which was near to that of Adriana and Armin on Fribourgstrasse, but he seldom talked about them or let them visit the school. Sometimes, he couldn't remember the name of the woman he was currently sleeping with. He said to Gustav, 'Perhaps one day it will be different, but for the moment, it isn't like that, any more than it is for you, eh, Gustav?'

'No,' said Gustav. 'I've got no time for it. My heart and mind are taken up entirely by the Hotel Perle.'

'There is a road'

IT WAS AN autumn day. There was bright foliage in the grounds of the Marburg Hospital, where crows strutted about on the lawn, under a fine blue sky. Among the crows was a single Canada goose. An elderly hospital resident was feeding the birds, but as they clustered round, she kept sending the goose away. 'Go away, goose!' she muttered. 'Come here, crows! Didn't you hear me, goose? Goose, go away!' And Gustav thought, yes, that is how life is always arranged, with one living thing being chosen over another, and the loser sent away to hunger and solitude.

Adriana and Anton were sitting on an iron bench. Adriana was reading to Anton from the Geneva newspaper, *Le Temps*. She was stylishly dressed, as ever, but Anton was wearing a faded hospital gown, with one of Adriana's shawls draped over it. His feet and legs were bare.

Gustav walked towards the bench and Anton turned and saw him. At once, Anton got up and stretched wide his arms, and when Gustav reached him, he clutched him in a tight embrace. 'Help me,' he whispered, 'help me. You're the only one who can.'

Gustav sat down on the bench with Anton and Adriana. Nobody spoke. Part of Gustav's attention kept returning to the old woman and the strutting crows. The goose was now standing apart.

After a moment, Adriana got up. She told Anton that she was going to leave him with Gustav and come back tomorrow. Anton replied that he hoped he wouldn't be at the hospital tomorrow. Adriana looked at him with sadness. Then she kissed his head, where a patch of hair had been torn out, and walked away.

Anton pulled his mother's shawl more closely round his body. Gustav asked him if he was cold.

'No,' he said. 'I know the winter's coming, but I don't feel the cold of the air. I only feel the storms inside me.'

Gustav stared at Anton's arms, scarred red where he'd slashed them. He imagined, for one terrible second, that all the wounds had been made by skate blades.

'You don't have to look at me,' Anton said. 'I know I look like a freak. But you have to help me. If you don't help me, I'm lost.'

Gustav waited. He took Anton's hand and held it in his and stroked it, like he used to stroke Lottie's hand when she talked about suicide.

Anton's eyes closed for a moment, as though the stroking soothed him. Then he said, 'Listen, Gustav. Are you listening? I have to go to Davos. You have to get me there. I can't be in Geneva and I can't go back to Matzlingen. You've got to get me to the sanatorium in the woods. What was its name?'

'Sankt Alban.'

'That's it: Sankt Alban. We left a tambourine on one of the beds. I need to go there now.'

Gustav waited, in case Anton had more to say, then he answered, 'I'm sure you can go to Davos, Anton. Provided we can find a hospital there which will take you . . .'

'No, no,' he said. 'Not a hospital. I need to go back to the Sankt Alban Sanatorium. I need to find the tambourine.'

'I don't think those things will be there any more, Anton, neither the tambourine nor the sanatorium.'

'Why not? We healed the dying there. Don't you remember? We laid the beds on the balcony. And the sunlight was strong and white. It will all be there.'

'It was a ruined place, Anton. Even then, it was a shell. It was only us who made it come alive.'

'So we'll make it come alive again. I need to wipe out time, you see. I need to get back to the place where I can start everything afresh. At first, I couldn't think where I could go. My world has shrunk so much. I can't stand to be anywhere. But then I remembered Davos and Sankt Alban. So you fix it up, Gustav. Right? And you have to come with me. I need you to answer when I bang the tambourine.'

Gustav waited a moment, then he said, 'I'll do my best to fix it up, Anton. But I have to know what I'm fixing in you first. You have to tell me what's happened to you.'

Anton shook his head. 'This is what everybody asks,' he said. 'What's happened to you? What's happened? But I don't want to talk about it. I *refuse* to answer that question. I just want to arrive at Sankt Alban and begin everything again. I'm depending on you, Gustav – only on you, out of everybody in the whole world! But if you can't fix it for me, tell me now and you can fuck off out of this place, whatever it is, and never see me alive again!'

'This place is a hospital, Anton,' said Gustav calmly. 'A very good hospital. If you stay here, you'll get well.'

'No, I won't. I'll kill myself. I thought you were my friend, Gustav. I thought you'd be on my side.'

'I am on your side. Goodness knows, Anton, I've been *on your side* for over fifty years! Can't you recognise that, by now?'

'Fifty years? Have we lived that long?'

'Yes.'

'Are we old?'

'Almost. We're getting that way.'

'That was probably why Hans betrayed me. I got too old.'

'Hans Hirsch betrayed you?'

'People make promises. But they're never kept. Everybody in the world betrays us – and then we betray ourselves. We cut our flesh . . . But if I can get to Davos, with you, and think myself back in time, when things were ordinary and safe, then I might have some hope of life.'

This phrase, *hope of life*, Gustav seemed to hear from a great distance, as though it came echoing through the sky. And he thought, would my own existence have been happier, if I'd never known Anton Zwiebel? And he felt, at this moment, that it would have been.

Although Emilie Perle had schooled him well in how to

love without being loved in return, he could now see how this state of lovelessness had made him obsessive in his quest for superficial order and control. He looked over at the old woman who had succeeded in separating the crows from the goose, and he wondered if he didn't, after all, resemble her in a mortifying way, wanting everything to be part of some category or other and never letting things be how they truly yearn to be. He saw that the goose was now sitting on its own on a concrete pathway, pecking at its own feathers.

GUSTAV STAYED WITH Anton until the light began to fade and a nurse came out and called Anton inside. She led him away and he went obediently, without saying goodbye to Gustav or turning round as he disappeared from sight.

THE FOLLOWING DAY, Adriana and Gustav went to see the director of the Marburg Hospital. When Gustav told him about Anton's expressed desire to go to Davos, the director said, 'Well, it's almost certainly delusionary. He's much better off here.'

Adriana said, 'I'm sorry, Herr Director, but why shouldn't Anton be moved to Davos, if that's his wish?'

The director gave Adriana one of those condescending smiles which, Gustav had often noted, seemed to be the speciality of people high up in the medical profession, and said, 'Davos was once a place renowned for its management of tuberculosis, as you probably know. But today, it's a winter sports resort. And the near association of illness is suicidal to tourism. So as far as I know, there are no suitable clinics in Davos to treat Anton's condition. I can enquire, but I'm not hopeful. The Marburg can help him, but you must understand that he's on a long road. We hope he will recover, but this will take time.'

'You *hope*,' said Adriana. 'You mean you're not certain he'll recover?'

'No. In cases like this one can never be certain. We do our best. But we're not helped by the fact that there seems to be nothing that Anton wants to *do*. He refuses all group therapy, becoming abusive if he's forced to participate in this. We've asked him to tell us how he'd like to pass the time, but –'

'Music,' said Adriana at once. 'He's a wonderful musician. I'm surprised you haven't heard his name.'

'Sorry, no,' said the director. 'What instrument does he play?'

'Piano. He's made recordings for the CavalliSound label. Beethoven sonatas.'

'Oh yes? Good for him. But of course we couldn't have him playing the piano here. It would be far too disruptive for the other patients.'

THE NEXT DAY, Gustav went to see Anton in his small room. He was lying on his bed, tugging at his hair. 'Shall I start packing, Gustav?' he asked at once. 'Have you arranged the travel to Davos?'

'No,' said Gustav. 'Davos has changed, Anton. It's a ski resort now. There's no clinic there which could look after you.'

'I don't want to go to a clinic,' said Anton, reaching out and clutching Gustav's arm. 'I told you. I want to go to Sankt Alban. I don't need shrinks and all that shit. You could look after me. All I need is that mountainside and a bed on a balcony and a view of what is to come.'

'What do you mean, "a view of what is to come"?'

'There is a road, Gustav. You know there is. Just this one road we have to take. We have to become the people we always should have been.'

Gustav stared down at Anton – his thin face, his bright and hectic eyes.

'I don't know what you mean,' Gustav said.

'Yes, you do. You knew what we should have been, but I was the one who resisted. Except that one time, at Sankt Alban, when I was the dying boy and you saved my life with a kiss. Now, you have to save it again.'

© David Kirkham

ROSE TREMAIN was born in London in 1943. She was sent away to boarding school at the age of ten where she discovered a love of writing and spent much of her free time scripting plays for her classmates to perform. After school she studied first at the Sorbonne in Paris before returning to England to study at UEA.

She worked as a script-reader, a teacher at a boys' prep school and an editor before becoming a full-time writer. Her first novel was published in 1976 and has been followed by thirteen further novels, five collections of short stories and a memoir, *Rosie*. She was one of only five women to be included in *Granta*'s original list of the 20 Best of Young British Novelists in 1983 and her books have won the Orange Prize, the Whitbread, the Prix Femina Etranger and the *Sunday Express* Book of the Year. As well as writing, she has helped launch the careers of several novelists, including Tracy Chevalier and Andrew Miller whom she taught at UEA and where she later became the first female Chancellor.

Rose lives in Norfolk with the biographer, Richard Holmes. She is the mother of one daughter, Eleanor and has two grandchildren, Archie and Martha. She was made a CBE in 2007.

RECOMMENDED BOOKS BY ROSE TREMAIN:

Merivel
The Road Home
Rosie

What sustains a Friendship?

Love
JEANETTE WINTERSON

VINTAGE MINIS

Language
XIAOLU GUO

VINTAGE MINIS

Desire
HARUKI MURAKAMI

VINTAGE MINIS

Freedom
MARGARET ATWOOD

VINTAGE MINIS

VINTAGE MINIS

The Vintage Minis bring you some of the world's greatest writers on the experiences that make us human. These stylish, entertaining little books explore the whole spectrum of life – from birth to death, and everything in between. Which means there's something here for everyone, whatever your story.

Desire	Haruki Murakami
Love	Jeanette Winterson
Marriage	Jane Austen
Babies	Anne Enright
Language	Xiaolu Guo
Motherhood	Helen Simpson
Fatherhood	Karl Ove Knausgaard
Summer	Laurie Lee
Jealousy	Marcel Proust
Sisters	Louisa May Alcott
Home	Salman Rushdie
Race	Toni Morrison
Liberty	Virginia Woolf
Swimming	Roger Deakin
Friendship	Rose Tremain
Work	Joseph Heller
Money	Yuval Noah Harari
Austerity	Yanis Varoufakis
Injustice	Richard Wright
War	Sebastian Faulks
Depression	William Styron
Drinking	John Cheever

vintageminis.co.uk